High-Wing Singles (pp.

FIXED GEAR

Tail-Draggers (pp. 50-73)

Tricycle (pp. 70-81)

RETRACTABLE

Tricycle (pp. 76-81)

Amphibians (pp. 82-89)

Twins (pp. 90-135)

SMALL

Low-Wing (pp. 90-111)

High-Wing (pp. 110-113)

Continued on back endpapers

A Field Guide
to Airplanes
of North America

A Field Guide to

Airplanes

of North America

M. R. Montgomery
and Gerald L. Foster

Illustrated by Gerald L. Foster

Houghton Mifflin Company · Boston
1984

Library of Congress Cataloging in Publication Data

Montgomery, M. R.
    A field guide to airplanes of North America.

    Bibliography: p.
    Includes index.
    1. Airplanes—Recognition.   I. Title
TL671.M58   1984   629.133'34   83-26438
ISBN 0-395-35313-0

Printed in the United States of America

M 10 9 8 7 6 5 4 3 2 1

Contents

Introduction

The purpose of this book is simple: to allow anyone interested in aviation to *identify* the factory-built, fixed-wing aircraft seen in North America. It is a field guide, not an encyclopedia or a history of aviation. The organizing principle is visual, and we have made every effort to ensure that airplanes that resemble one another are grouped—if not on the same page, then within a page or two.

A few airplane identification books were published before Houghton Mifflin decided to expand its Field Guide program to include manmade objects, but we believe this book is unique. Like the Peterson Field Guides, it is devoted to a specific geographical area—North America, in this case. Although nearly all the airplanes in this book can be seen anywhere in the world, we have eliminated the foreign aircraft you're not likely to encounter. Guides to "all the world" are forced to eliminate many of the rarer and older planes, as they are obliged to lump the many similar models of one manufacturer (the Piper Cherokee, for example) into a rather indistinct and blurred composite airplane. We have tried, in these complex families of airplanes, to make subtler distinctions. In the first few pages, for example, four different models of the Waco biplane are illustrated. In general, this is a book of native and naturalized airplanes. Just as bird guides do not include exotic birds found in zoological parks, this guide does not include museum pieces.

No field guide could cover every airplane that can be seen in North America, for there still exist specimens, or newly manufactured replicas, of practically every plane built since, and including, the Wright Brothers' Flyer. We used two principles in selecting more than 300 airplanes for inclusion in the book. First, we have included all airplanes for which 35 or more specimens are currently flying. Second, we have tried to include every passenger plane on which it is still possible, or will soon be possible, to buy a ticket.

A single large class of fixed-wing aircraft not exhaustively covered here is the "home-builts"; their variety is simply too great and the confusion among them too likely. Almost all of the home-builts are easily recognized as such: They are quite small, often seating only one person, and they look "experimental." The best source for information on home-builts, as on many other subjects, is *Jane's All the World's Aircraft*. Issues of *Jane's* have, for the past few years, included a separate section on home-builts and other amateur experimental aircraft. Nevertheless, our book, though almost entirely devoted to commercially manufactured aircraft, does mention a few home-built biplanes. There are literally hundreds of them, sometimes thousands, and they closely resemble, and are often patterned after, production biplanes of the 1930s. We hope their inclusion here will help clarify the difference between production and home-built biplanes.

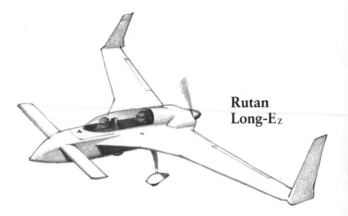

Rutan Long-Ez

One other class of home-built aircraft deserves to be mentioned here. Two manufacturers have sold thousands of kits for aircraft that have a small wing forward and a larger wing to the rear: the canard wing (from the French word for duck, so called because the rear placement of the larger wing gives the canard aircraft a long-necked look). This is hardly a new design; the Wright Flyer had a smaller wing forward of its large biplane wings. The two most common canard wings are the Rutan Long-Ez, with its pusher propeller, and the slightly more conventional-looking Quickie (also designed by Burt Rutan), with its puller propeller. Each is capable of cruising at 180 mph (290 km/h). The combination of pusher propeller(s) and double lifting surfaces has moved from the home-built personal aircraft to the business market with several new aircraft under development as this book goes to press. They are included in the chapter titled "New Generation Pusher-Props."

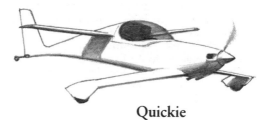

Quickie

How to Use This Book

The airplanes are grouped by type and appearance. Conventional aircraft are grouped by their physical similarity. All the conventional biplanes are together, followed by agricultural biplanes, followed by single-wing agricultural planes. (All planes built specifically for crop dusting and spraying are easily recognized by their roll-bar-protected cockpit.)

Single-engine propeller-driven planes are grouped by such quickly visible field marks as whether they have wings mounted on the top of the fuselage or on the bottom and whether their landing gear is the fixed, tail-dragging type, the type with a fixed tricycle gear with a nose wheel, or the retractable type. Several manufacturers made airplanes that are identical except for having two or more types of landing gear; these airplanes will be found in the transitional pages between one group and the next.

Both the twin-propeller and the multijet airplanes are separated into different groups by their size. Any rigid plan—keeping all twin, fuselage-mounted, swept-wing jets together regardless of size, for example—would have put something as large as a stretched DC9 next to a much smaller, not at all similar, Falcon 20 business jet that seats eight.

Chapter 10, "Military Aircraft," illustrates *special-purpose* aircraft in U.S. and Canadian service. With the exception of a few basic trainers, their shapes are all so unusual as to be quickly distinguished from commercial and general aviation planes. The order is from single-engine propeller through multi-engine, and then single jet engines through multijet aircraft. "Level flight" speeds indicate official information on the plane's maximum speed, excluding dives; it is probably underestimated. Mach numbers are decimal proportions of the speed of sound at the altitude where the airspeed of the plane has been measured. Current usage is to drop the hyphen between the manufacturer's acronym and the model number. We have followed that for civilian aircraft (e.g., DC9 refers to Douglas Aircraft model number 9), but we've kept the hyphen for military designations, providing a quick visual distinction in the text and index.

Note, however, that the military services of both countries acquire, from time to time, various civilian airplanes for non-combat purposes, especially for transporting VIPs in more than ordinary military comfort. Conventional-looking aircraft with military insignia should be looked for in other sections of this book, according to the general principles of arrangement.

Several commercial airliners have been acquired by the military, including: the Boeing 737-200 (page 158), flown as the T-43A navigation trainer; the Boeing 707 (page 160), as a VIP transport (of which the best known is Air Force 1) and as in-flight refueling tankers in the U.S. and as a utility transport in Canada; the Boeing 747 (page 162) as the E-4A "Airborne Command Post" by the U.S. Strategic Air Command. Douglas DC10s (page 156) are flown as KC-10A Extender air-to-air refueling craft in the U.S., and the DC9 (page 154) is in service as a flying ambulance/hospital as the C-9A Nightingale, in a VIP transport role as the VC-9A.

Smaller civilian jets in military service are the Lockheed Jetstar (page 148) (the C-140 in U.S. service), the North American Rockwell Sabreliner (page 146) (as the CT-39 VIP transport), and the French-built Falcon 20 (page 146) (as the HU-25 search plane in the U.S. Coast Guard and as the CC-117 transport in Canada).

Propeller planes in service include the de Havilland Dash 7 (page 136) (in Canada as the CC-132 troop transport); the DC3 (in Canada, the C-47 Dakota); the Convair 540 (page 126) (used in the U.S. Coast Guard as the C-131 Samaritan and in Canada as the CC-109 Cosmopolitan); and the de Havilland Twin Otter (page 112) and single-engine Otters (page 50) (in several government departments in both countries as transport, observation, and search-and-rescue planes).

Both countries use standard civilian aircraft as primary flight trainers, the high-wing Cessna 172s (page 76) in the U.S. and the low-wing Beech Musketeer (page 28) in Canada.

We have avoided, as much as possible, any technical language. There are, however, two useful field marks on airplanes that do have their own special words. The best way to describe a wing that is the same width along its entire length is to refer to its "constant chord" (from the word used in geometry to describe a straight line drawn across the underside of a curve). Airplane wings are typically curved over the top and relatively flat on the bottom, where the "chord" measurement is made.

The other necessary technical word is "dihedral," which describes wings, or tail planes, that are bent upward so that the wing tip is higher than the root of the wing as it leaves the fuselage. Even very slight dihedrals are quite noticeable and make good field marks. The Martin 404 airliner, for example, is recognizable at a considerable distance because it is unique, among all the twin-prop airliners, in having a dihedral in both the wing and the tail plane.

In place of the more technical "vertical stabilizer" and "horizontal stabilizer," we have used "tail fin" and "tail plane." The little mudguard fenders on fixed-gear wheels we simply call "wheel pants" (the more accurate British slang for them is "wheel spats"). The word "fairing," which appears often, is an old word from ship architecture that simply means a smoothed-out or streamlined connection between parts of the airplane. Fairings are typical at the leading edges of wings and tail surfaces, and where engines are mounted on wings. Streamlined engine housings are called "nacelles" (from an old French word meaning "little boat," which captures their general tapering shape quite accurately).

Identifying a particular aircraft usually requires noting a *combination* of two or more field marks. For some of the most similar models (and American manufacturers turn out a dizzying number of nearly identical aircraft), you may be reduced to observing the number and shape of passenger windows or to trying to catch a glimpse of other field marks equally difficult to see when the plane is high overhead. The best place to identify airplanes is at an airport. Watch them as they taxi on the runway, make the identification, and then watch closely as they disappear into the distance. Once you have seen the plane, learned its name, and watched it fly a few times, many of our field marks will become irrelevant. Almost all planes have a unique "presence"—"gestalt," in psychological jargon—which is more important than the smaller field marks once you're familiar with the plane. Just as you can recognize people you know far beyond the distance at which you can see the color of their eyes or the shape of their nose—any of their personal field marks—so it is with many aircraft. The first time or two you may have to count the windows or the passenger doors to separate a "stretched" DC8 from another four-jet airliner. But once you know that plane, with its long, skinny fuselage perched on improbably small wings, it will be recognizable at several miles.

There is no rigid order for using the field marks. We suggest you thumb through the sections of high-wing or low-wing single-engine aircraft and note the *kinds* of field marks; then learn to look for them all at once. This will work better than some sort of litany of "wing, tail, landing gear, windows." Familiarity with this book is the best system.

A Field Guide
to Airplanes
of North America

Beech BE17 Staggerwing
(Navy GB-1, Air Force C-43)

Length: 26'9" (8.13 m)   *Wingspan:* 32' (9.76 m)   *Cruising speed:* 201 mph (323 km/h)

Rare. Large; *reversed staggerwing (lower wing forward of upper); enclosed cabin; solid wing struts.*

The Rolls-Royce of biplanes. Performance data is for the most powerful versions, with 450-horsepower engines. First flown in 1932 with fixed landing gear; never seen today without the electrically operated retractable gear. Various models have slight dimensional changes, but all are clearly Staggerwings. Once a popular float and ski plane. A few postwar models, last produced in 1948, have leather upholstery and other comforts.

Note: Any cabin biplane that is not a Beech 17 (reversed staggerwing) is a Waco.

Any cabin biplane with an upper wing much longer and deeper than the bottom wing is a late-model Waco C (custom) biplane.

All other cabin biplanes, with wings of equal width and normal stagger are Waco S (standard) or very early C (custom) planes.

Waco Late C Series

Length: 27'7" (8.42 m)   *Wingspan:* upper, 34'9" (10.57 m); lower, 24'6" (7.47 m)   *Cruising speed:* 155 mph (249 km/h)

Rare. A *cabin biplane* with a *noticeably shorter and narrower lower wing* (compare with Waco S series, below); *fixed landing gear; N wing struts,* plus a *heavy brace* from the base of the N strut to the upper wing.

One of four basic types of Waco biplanes, the late C (custom cabin) series is the only one with the very small, normally staggered lower wing. Built throughout the 1930s. The fixed gear is usually seen with streamlined wheel pants. Proper restoration includes the straight-line striping from the engine cowling to the tail plane. A few were in U.S. and foreign military service, but for the famous WWII basic trainer see PT-14, next page .

Waco S Series, Early C Series

Length: 25'3" (7.71 m)   *Wingspan:* upper, 33'3" (10.15 m); lower, 28'3" (8.62 m)   *Cruising speed:* 133 mph (214 km/h)

Rare. *Cabin biplane* with *slightly shorter lower wing;* wings of *equal width (chord); N struts, plus solid brace.*

The S (standard) and early C (custom) Waco biplanes are handsome, symmetrical, and remarkable for their lack of unusual features. They have very similar upper and lower wings, typical struts, and a conventional cabin. Usually restored with the Waco signature stripe from cowling to tail. Both wings have a matching, very slight dihedral. Although they were not supplied with streamlined wheel pants, like the C series, you may see one that's been modified. Concentrate on the wings.

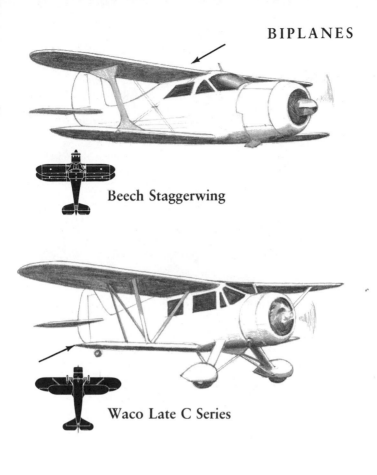

BIPLANES

Beech Staggerwing

Waco Late C Series

Waco S Series

Boeing/Stearman Kaydet
(military PT-13, PT-17, PT-18)

Length: 24'10" (7.58 m)   *Wingspan:* upper, 32'2" (9.82 m); lower,
1' shorter overall   *Cruising speed:* 103 mph (166 km/h)

Fairly common. The *normally staggered wings of almost equal
length,* combined with the *unbraced heavy landing gear* and the *N
struts without an aileron connector,* separate the Kaydet from the
somewhat similar biplanes of the 1930s and 1940s. Compare the
three aircraft that follow below.

More than 10,000 Stearmans were built from the early 1930s
through WWII; model designators indicate engines of different
horsepower. A jointly procured trainer for the Navy and the Army
Air Corps, many are seen restored to their WWII paint scheme—
Air Force blue fuselage and Navy yellow wings with service markings. Note that although the cockpits are large and deep, there is
no turtleback behind the rear cockpit.

Naval Aircraft Factory N3N1, N3N3

Length: 25'11" (7.96 m)   *Wingspan:* 34' (10.38 m)   *Cruising
speed:* 92 mph (148 km/h)

Rare. *Normally staggered wings identical in length and width
(chord); N struts* with *aileron connector; skinny braced landing
gear without wheel pants; no engine cowling.*

Once used extensively as agricultural aircraft, the government-
built N3Ns are collectors' items. A proper restoration is all yellow
with Navy insignia. The last biplane in U.S. service, until 1958, as
a float plane at the U.S. Naval Academy, Annapolis. All midship-
men had to spend ten hours flying in the "Yellow Peril" whether
they were aviators or not—for many, an experience that was
equaled only by submarine escape training for sheer terror.

Waco UPF7, YPF7 (military trainer PT-14),
Model D

Length: 23'1" (7.06 m)   *Wingspan:* upper, 30' (9.14 m); lower,
26'10" (8.18 m)   *Cruising speed:* 123 mph (198 km/h)

Fairly common. *Lower wing noticeably shorter;* look for the
large rectangular cutout in the upper wing; designed for easier access to the forward cockpit; *longer nosed* than the early F series;
may or may not have engine cowling.

Although a military trainer in WWII, not as common as the
Stearman Kaydets or the Naval Factory N3N series. Very popular
primary trainer with the WWII government Civilian Pilot Training
Program. A sports type (Waco model D) was built with streamlined wheel pants and lighter construction materials.

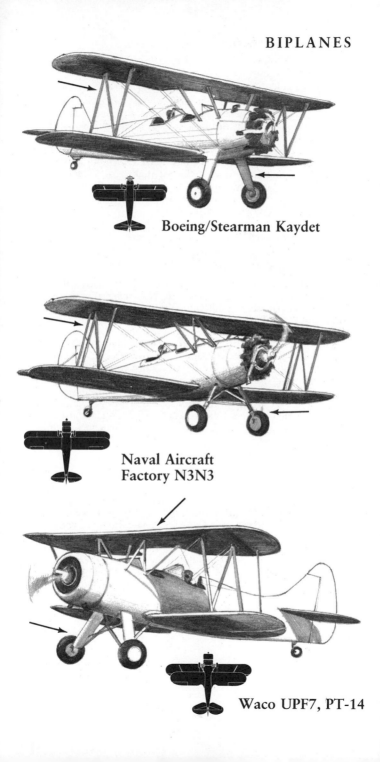

BIPLANES

Boeing/Stearman Kaydet

Naval Aircraft
Factory N3N3

Waco UPF7, PT-14

Waco Early F Series

Length: 20'9" (6.31 m)   *Wingspan:* 29'6" (9 m)   *Cruising speed:* 90 mph (145 km/h)

Rare. May be confused with the Waco UPF7 or the naval aircraft trainer, *but very stubby nosed; wings of equal length; N brace* with *aileron connector; small circular cutout in top wing* for access to front cockpit; distinct turtleback behind rear cockpit. Compare Waco old F above.

A popular sportster and trainer from the early 1930s, the early F series is popular with restorers, but much less common than the Waco UPF7 military trainers, which it slightly resembles. Built with and without engine cowlings, some with ring cowlings, some with streamlined cowling, but typically with exposed radial engine cylinder heads. Landing gear usually bare.

Travel Air 4000

Length: 24'2" (7.35 m)   *Wingspan:* 34'8" (10.53 m)   *Cruising speed:* 100 mph (161 km/h)

Rare. *Looks distinctly antique;* almost always shows the *elephant-ear upper wing tip and tail fin; N bracing,* plus aileron control transfer bar; some built with conventional speed wings, but these show the elephant-ear tail; a few with conventionally rounded tails, but these always show the upper wing elephant ear, which is an extension of the aileron; both wings straight, lower wing noticeably shorter and slightly narrower.

The Travel Air was built in a variety of versions, including passenger carriers, with a two-man forward cockpit. All originals and accurate restorations have either radial (in the more numerous 4000 series) or in-line (in the very rare 2000 series) water-cooled engines. A small radiator extends below the fuselage, just forward of the cockpit area. The high, quickly rising turtleback is unique.

Fleet Finch Trainer

Length: 21'8" (7.1 m)   *Wingspan:* both, 28' (8.53 m)   *Cruising speed:* 98 mph (158 km/h)

Rare. *Very stubby nosed; straight wings of equal length; lower wing with noticeable dihedral; N bracing; no aileron control* transfer bar. Early models, built in the U.S., have elephant-ear tails.

Made in the U.S. in the early 1930s, then in Canada, where more than 600 were built from 1938 to 1941 for RCAF flight training. Many restored Canadian-built WWII trainers have a single sliding canopy that covers both cockpits; other models have simple, flat-glass, three-sided windshields. Once a popular ski and float plane.

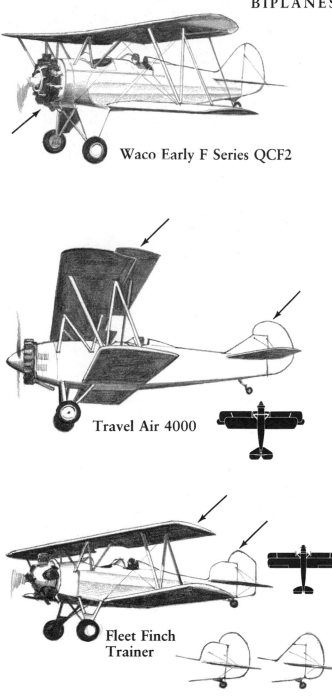

BIPLANES

Waco Early F Series QCF2

Travel Air 4000

Fleet Finch
Trainer

Meyers OTW

Length: 22'8" (6.91 m)   *Wingspan:* both, 30' (9.14 m)   *Cruising speed:* 100 mph (161 km/h)

Rare. Combines *all-aluminum fuselage* with *fabric wings;* wings are identical, with slight dihedral; *the landing gear strut shock-absorbing piston,* which extends up to the forward cockpit, *is diagnostic.*

Only 102 "Out to Wins" were built during WWII, all for the Civilian Pilot Training Program, and half of them are still registered—some flying, the others being restored. Their use as crop dusters after WWII contributed to the loss of many of the aircraft. Manufactured in Romulus, Michigan, from 1940 to 1944 by people who had never before, and never afterward, built airplanes.

de Havilland DH82 Tiger Moth

Length: 23'11" (7.29 m)   *Wingspan:* 29'4" (8.94 m)   *Cruising speed:* 90 mph (145 km/h)

Fairly common for an antique biplane. *Swept wings of equal length; stout double-bar wing connectors (not N);* the entire plane gives a distinct impression of slimness, including the in-line engine and the fancifully tapered tail fin and tail planes. Compare with the chubbier Bucker Jungmeister.

The Tiger Moth, a 130-horsepower version of the 1920s Gipsy Moth, first flew in 1932 and was produced through WWII, totaling more than 8000 planes. The standard RAF and Royal Navy primary trainer; a few hundred in USAAF, designated PT-24. Surplus Moths were the backbone of private aviation in Great Britain and Canada after WWII. The bulky apparatus over the cockpit that connects the left and right wings is the fuel tank, and another good way of distinguishing the Moths from the Jungmeister.

Bucker Jungmann, Jungmeister

Jungmann specifications: *Length:* 21'8" (6.60 m)   *Wingspan:* 24'3" (7.40 m)   *Cruising speed:* 106 mph (171 km/h)

There are single- (Jungmeister) and dual-control (Jungmann) craft, but all share these field marks: *strongly swept wings of equal length,* with *double wing struts. Compare tail plane and fin with Tiger Moth.* Single-seaters have radial engines, two-seaters have in-lines. Concentrate on the wing and tail combination. The much smaller, similarly shaped Pitts Special has a single wing strut.

First built in the mid-1930s, the Jungmeister and Jungmann trained Hitler's Luftwaffe; built in several countries before WWII, and re-created by several companies after the war; a few in Japanese Air Force during WWII; the most maneuverable and acrobatic of all the pre–WWII biplanes: War surplus models dominated acrobatic flying in the 1950s. There are also a few home-built 8/10 scale models in service.

BIPLANES

Meyers OTW

de Havilland
Tiger Moth

Bucker Jungmann

Bucker Jungmeister

Great Lakes Sport Trainer, Baby Lakes

Great Lakes specifications: *Length:* 20'4" (6.2 m)   *Wingspan:* 26'8" (8.13 m)   *Cruising speed:* 110 mph (177 km/h). Baby Lakes specifications: *Length:* 13'9" (4.10 m)   *Wingspan:* 16'8" (5.08 m) *Cruising speeds:* various, depending on optional engines

The original Great Lakes, built between 1929 and 1932, and the revival, built between 1974 and 1978, were tandem dual controls; the Baby Lakes is 6/10 their size and is either single or dual. They share the identifying combination: *top wing swept, over straight bottom wing and N struts.* Owners can modify struts to a single one, thereby possibly causing confusion with the Pitts Special (next entry). Call it a Pitts/Lake, especially if the wheel struts on the Great Lakes have been covered with streamlining sheet metal. Original Great Lakes had ailerons on the lower wing only; some have been modified and show the aileron transfer control bar next to the N brace.

Although only 200 of the original Great Lakes trainers were built, they dominated acrobatics and closed-course racing in the U.S. in the 1930s. The company was revived and several versions, of greatly varying horsepower, were built. You may even see a one-seat, full-size Great Lakes. Concentrate on the wing and wing strut combination. It's unique.

Pitts S-1, S-2 Special

S-1 specifications: *Length:* 15'5" (4.7 m)   *Wingspan:* 17'4" (5.28 m)   *Cruising speed:* 140 mph (225 km/h)

Usually seen in the S-1 (single-seat) version. A chunky little plane. The unique combination is *top wing swept and slightly longer than straight lower wing; single wing strut plus aileron control transfer bar. Optional fuselage/upper wing bracing may originate from two points on the wing rather than the typical N bracing.* The turtleback is high and distinctive.

The single-seat S-1 is unique in that it is available as a factory-built and certified plane or as plans or kits for the home builder. The S-2 dual control is only available through the factory. They have been flown with all manner of engines, up to 450 horsepower; supplanted the Jungmeister as the premier aerobatic airplane in the 1960s. Home-built Pitts Specials may show additional bracing and wiring, probably out of a deep sense of insecurity on the part of the builder.

Christen Eagle I, II

Eagle II (two-seater) specifications: *Length:* 18'6" (5.64 m) *Wingspan:* 19'11" (6.07 m)   *Cruising speed:* 158 mph (254 km/h)

A kit-builder's plane. The one-seat Eagle I, introduced in late 1982, has *both wings swept, single strut, and bubble canopy.* It's almost always seen with Eagle paint job, *long-nosed, large propeller spinner.*

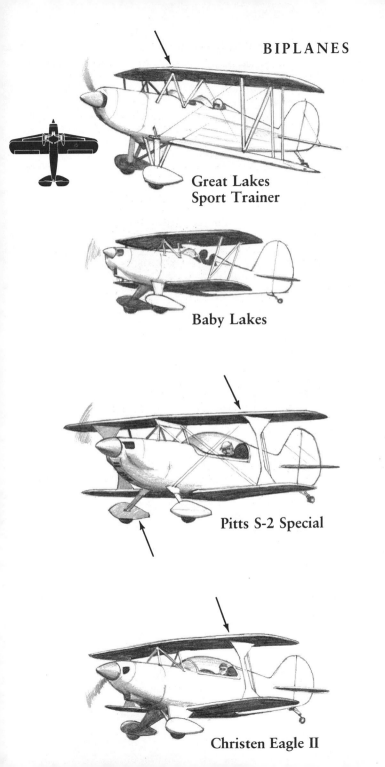

BIPLANES

Great Lakes
Sport Trainer

Baby Lakes

Pitts S-2 Special

Christen Eagle II

Stolp Starduster, Acroduster

Starduster 100 specifications: *Length:* 16'6" (5.03 m)   *Wingspan:*
upper, 19' (5.79 m); lower, 18' (5.49 m)   *Cruising speed:*
132 mph (212 km/h)

A family of home-builts. The Stardusters and the more strongly
constructed aerobatic Acrodusters have *unequal span wings.* Only
the *upper wing is swept;* single interplane strut and aileron transfer
control bar, *fully rounded wing tips.* Also seen in two-seaters; separates from same-sized Christen Eagles by the asymmetry of the
wings. See the similar Steen Skybolt (next entry) and note its less
rounded wing tips.

Steen Skybolt

Length: 19' (5.79 m)   *Wingspan:* upper, 24' (7.32 m); lower, 23'
(7.01 m)   *Cruising speed:* 130 mph (209 km/h)

Always a two-seater. *Upper wing swept, lower straight; very
long-nosed, large rounded tail fin. Wing braces over the fuselage
radiate from two points on the wing.* Compare the more conventional combination N braces on a Stolp Starduster. Sold as plans,
with wing and fuselage kits available. More than 2500 kits have
been sold.

Smith Miniplane

Length: 15'3" (4.65 m)   *Wingspan:* upper, 17' (5.18 m); lower,
15'9" (4.80 m)   *Cruising speed:* 118 mph (190 km/h)

Properly called "mini." Small size; *wings not swept; lower wing
slightly shorter; conventional N bracing.* The first models were
known as DSA-1 (for Darn Small Airplane). Compare with the
very similar EAA Biplane (next entry). EAAs tend to have a more
streamlined engine cowling and a more upright tail fin.

EAA Biplane

Length: 17' (5.18 m)   *Wingspan:* both, 20' (6.10 m)   *Cruising
speed:* 110 mph (177 km/h)

A small, single-seat with *unswept, equal-length wings* and conventional *N struts.* A subtle difference between the EAA Biplane
and the Smith Miniplane is the way the lower wing appears to
come out of the EAA fuselage; in the Smith Mini the fuselage appears to sit on top of the wing. The Smith Mini has a noticeably
shorter lower wing.

EAA Acro-Sport, Acro-Sport II

Acro-Sport (single-seater) specifications: *Length:* 17'6" (5.33 m)
Wingspan: upper, 19'7" (5.97 m); lower, 19'1" (5.82 m)
Cruising speed: 105 mph (169 km/h)

The only biplane illustrated here with *unswept wings of nearly
equal length and a single streamlined strut, plus aileron control
transfer bar.* Designed to be built from plans and construction
manuals. More than 800 have been built and flown.

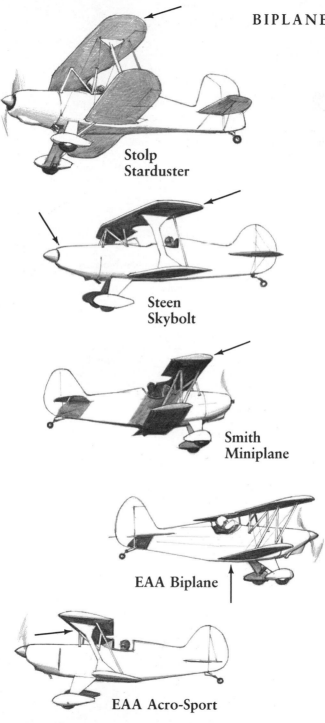

BIPLANES

Stolp
Starduster

Steen
Skybolt

Smith
Miniplane

EAA Biplane

EAA Acro-Sport

Eagle Aircraft Eagle 220, 300

Length: 27'6" (8.38 m)   *Wingspan:* 55' (16.76 m)   *Working speed:* 65–115 mph (105–185 km/h)

Not common. A 1981 introduction: *A biplane with extremely long, thin wings.* The typical agplane cockpit sits amid a maze of wires, struts, and braces; *large tail fin.*

A revival from the era when biplanes dominated the agricultural spraying industry, this Bellanca-designed agplane has an aspect totally different from the old biplanes converted to spraying: The wings are based on sailplane designs, long, thin, and tapering. More than 90 were produced by mid-1983. Earliest versions (not illustrated) used a radial engine, and the total length was only 26 feet (7.92 m). Current models are in-line pistons; model numbers (220, 300) indicate horsepower.

Schweitzer (Grumman) Ag-Cat

Length: 25'7" (7.80 m)   *Wingspan:* 42'3" (12.88 m)   *Working speed:* 98 mph (158 km/h)

Separate this biplane-agplane from older biplanes converted to crop use by its *massive, high tail fin; all-metal skin; modern roll-bar cockpit; and trimmed speed-wing wing tips.*

The original Ag-Cat was designed by Grumman but never manufactured until Schweitzer, a family-run designer of sailplanes, started manufacturing them under license from Grumman in 1957. Since 1981, Schweitzer has been the sole owner of the design, now marketing an Ag-Cat B with a standard 600-horsepower radial engine. When one considers this class of agricultural planes—many (like the Schweitzer) with pressurized cockpits to keep aerial sprays and dusts away from the pilot, air conditioning, and airframes meant to collapse slowly around a rigid cockpit in the case of a crash—one ceases to wonder why there are very few old, bold crop dusters. Compare these planes with the Call-Air A2 (next entry) where the pilot simply put a barrel of pesticide in the passenger's seat and took off.

AGRICULTURAL PLANES

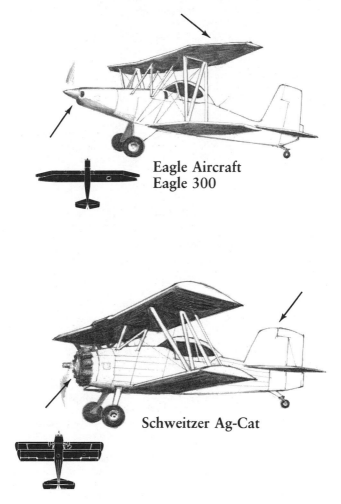

**Eagle Aircraft
Eagle 300**

Schweitzer Ag-Cat

Call-Air A2, A5

Length: 23'5" (7.25 m)   *Wingspan:* 36' (11.11 m)   *Cruising speed:* 102 mph (164 km/h)

Extremely rare, and probably permanently parked in a quiet part of the airfield. The *only production passenger aircraft with a low, braced wing.* Wing is constant chord (width) with rounded tips; three-strut landing gear usually has two struts covered with speed pants. Compare with the Intermountain Call-Air A9 agricultural plane (next entry).

Fewer than 50 built as passenger planes, a few more as Call-Air A5 and A6 crop dusters, with spray material carried inside the A2-style cabin; included here because its use of the constant-chord wing with high-lift qualities was unique when the plane was designed in 1939. Built in Wyoming at an airfield with an elevation of 6200 feet, the Call-Air was perfectly at home in "high and hot" thin air.

Intermountain Mfg. Co. Call-Air A9
Aero Commander Sparrow, Quail, Snipe
AAM Thrush Commander

Length: 24' (7.32 m)   *Wingspan:* 35' (10.67 m)   *Working speed:* 100 mph (161 km/h)

Not so common as some agricultural planes, but still being produced in Mexico by Aeronautica Agricola Mexicana. *Typical agplane shape, low wing braced with three struts, equal-chord (width) wings, light wire braces on tail planes, triple braces to forward wheels,* somewhat old-fashioned *curved tail fin and tail planes.* A rare Snipe model has a radial engine.

Agplane fans will see the family history of the Call-Air A9 in the triple wing braces and triple wheel struts, picked up from the original Call-Air A2 monoplane (above) and the now very rare Call-Air A5 and A6 agplanes. A Wyoming company developed the Call-Air A9 and manufactured a few hundred from 1963 to 1965. That design was sold to Aero Commander (a division of Rockwell—later, North American Rockwell). The A9 design survives today in the triple braces to the front wheels in the Thrush agplanes, which have a modern unbraced wing. Rockwell sold off the braced-wing design to Aeronautica Agricola Mexicana, which has continuously produced them at the rate of about two a month since 1978 and which has designated them AAM Thrush Commander and Sparrow Commander. A few of the earliest Call-Air A9s did not have windows in the roof of the cockpit. Close at hand, note the distinct droop to the leading edge of the wing, giving the plane a very short takeoff roll (1200 feet) when fully loaded.

AGRICULTURAL PLANES

Call-Air A2, A5

Call-Air A9

**Aero Commander
Quail**

Piper PA25 Pawnee

Length: 24' (7.32 m)   *Wingspan:* 36'2" (11.02 m)   *Working speed:* 95 mph (153 km/h)

A small, old-fashioned-looking agplane is either a Pawnee or one of the Sparrow Commander/Call-Air A9 types; compare with them before deciding. *Low wing has a pair of braces on top, tail planes with paired braces top and bottom, wings are fabric over rib, and it usually shows up clearly, rounded wing tips, rounded tail geometry.*

One of the first pure agplanes; built between 1959 and 1982; early replacement for the old biplane dusters. The high placement of the pilot, the rear cockpit windows, and the extra-long nose for progressive collapse if crashed, plus interior safety features, were designed in on the advice of Cornell University agricultural and mechanical engineering studies.

Cessna Ag Truck, Ag Wagon, Ag Pickup, Ag Husky

Length: 25'3" (7.70 m)   *Wingspan:* 40'4" (12.30 m)   *Working speed:* variable, about 100 mph (161 km/h)

Quite variable window configurations, but always with these constants: *Wing is braced by a single, streamlined strut that is faired into the wing; unbraced tail planes; single, spring-steel struts to front wheels; very sharp (9-degree) dihedral that begins after the wing leaves the fuselage horizontally.*

Developed in 1965, the Cessna Ag series has a number of names signifying nothing more than varieties of engines, load-carrying capacity, and variations in windows—many early models before 1969 lacked the rear and top cockpit windows. A few models beginning in 1971 had high-lift drooped wing tips. All models (and other Cessna singles) since 1980 have the conical camber wing tips.

Piper PA36 Brave, Pawnee Brave
WTA New Brave

Length: 27'6" (8.38 m)   *Wingspan:* 38'9" (11.83 m)   *Working speed:* 112 mph (180 km/h)

Typical agricultural low-wing monoplane. *Unbraced wings* (compare Thrush and Air Tractor, next entries); *wings of equal chord* (after fairing at wing root); *unbraced tail plane; forward landing gear struts are streamlined; shock absorbing; squared-off shape to tail fin, wing tips, and tail planes.*

Developed by Piper in 1972, now manufactured by WTA, Inc., a Texas company that also continues production of the Piper PA18 Super Cub. The extra-long nose of the Brave is so designed to collapse progressively in case of a crash. Not manufactured with radial engines or in two-seat models (compare the Thrush and Air Tractor).

AGRICULTURAL PLANES

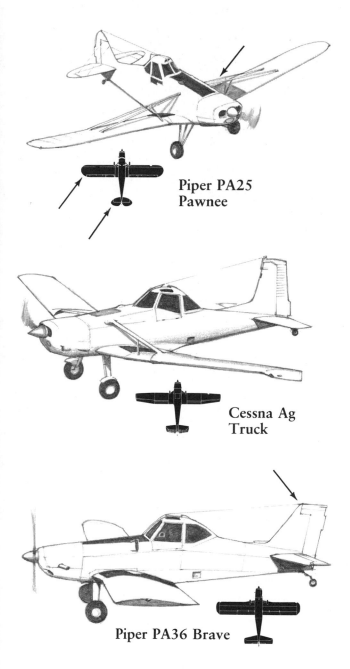

Piper PA25
Pawnee

Cessna Ag
Truck

Piper PA36 Brave

Ayres Thrush, Bull Thrush, Turbo Thrush
Rockwell-Commander Thrush

Length: 29'5" (8.96 m)   *Wingspan:* 44'5" (13.54 m)   *Working speed:* 110 mph (177 km/h)

Typical agricultural low-wing monoplane with *unbraced wings,* compare the Air Tractor (next entry) before deciding; *fixed gear; three struts for each forward wheel; pair of thin wire braces above and below tail planes; equal-chord (width) wings, with trapezoidal tips.*

Developed by Rockwell-Commander in 1965, manufactured by the Ayres Corporation since then. Comes in a variety of configurations, but all have the same field marks. The original models came with radial engines; recently with in-line turboprop engines (top picture). A two-seat cabin is standard on the 1200-horsepower radial Bull Thrush (bottom sketch), but is also available on the turboprop airframe. Bull Thrush carries up to 510 gallons of liquid spray.

Air Tractor

Length: 27' (8.23 m)   *Wingspan:* 45'1" (13.75 m)   *Working speed:* 130 mph (209 km/h)

Typical low-wing agricultural plane. *Unbraced wing,* compare the Thrush (previous entry) before deciding; *fixed gear; single, spring-steel strut carries each wheel; wing of equal chord (depth), with straight squared-off wing tips; pair of light braces on the underside only of the tail plane.*

Manufactured in various models since 1972. The field marks are consistent, although the plane is equipped with radial engines (model 301, lower sketch) or turboprop engines (model 302, 400, main drawing); designed by Leland Snow, who also designed the Snow S2 agplanes, which became the Rockwell Thrush, now the Ayres Thrush. It is *not* manufactured in a two-seater (compare the Thrush).

Weatherly 620, 620TP, 201

Length: 27'3" (8.30 m)   *Wingspan:* 41' (12.5 m)   *Working speed:* 105 mph (169 km/h)

Not common, and quite variable. All models have *low, unbraced wing of constant chord* (width); *very strong dihedral begins a few feet out from fuselage; top of triangular tail fin is clipped.* An option is detachable vanes that extend the spray path by about 8 feet (2.47 m).

Weatherly Aviation began by converting Fairchild M62 aircraft to crop sprayers, and continued with their own modifications of that design. Except for the radial engines on some models (bottom sketch) the plane has an air of angularity about it that is unique, including the constant-chord wings, the delta tail fin, and the trapezoidal tail planes. Even the tapers in the fuselage section appear to be flat sections.

AGRICULTURAL PLANES

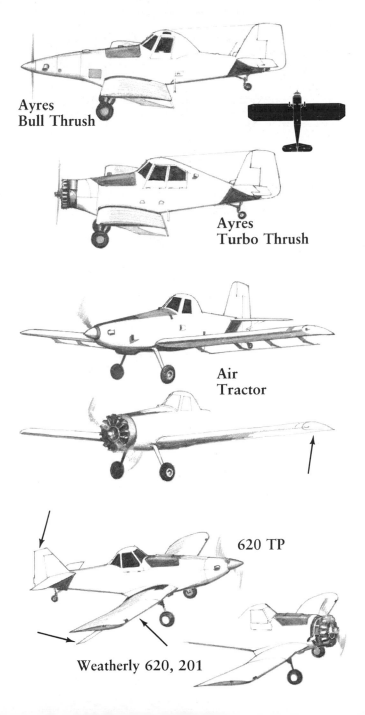

**Ayres
Bull Thrush**

**Ayres
Turbo Thrush**

**Air
Tractor**

620 TP

Weatherly 620, 201

Ryan ST3 (PT-21, PT-22 NR-1), Ryan ST

Length: 22'5" (6.83 m)   *Wingspan:* 30'1" (9.18 m)   *Cruising speed:* 123 mph (198 km/h)

Quite rare. *Constant-chord* (width); *low wing; rounded tips;* both the wings and tail planes are braced, top and bottom, with wire; *cylinder heads of the standard engine project through cowling; distinct, abrupt turtleback to rear cockpit.*

Of the thousands built, more than 500 PT-21s survived WWII training duties and entered the civilian market. Although slow, the plane was more than strong enough for acrobatics (the point of the noisy wire bracing). The plane had a fairly high stall speed, 64 mph (103 km/h), and sank like a rock without power. The civil version (ST) had an in-line engine and wheel pants (see sketch); the military five-banger was easier to work on, and the wheel pants were dropped in deference to the abuse landing gears took from student pilots.

Fairchild PT-19 (M62)

Length: 27'8" (8.5 m)   *Wingspan:* 35'11" (11 m)   *Cruising speed:* 120 mph (193 km/h)

Rare old birds. *Unbraced low wing; twin tandem cockpits* (which may be enclosed in a greenhouse, top sketch); *fixed taildragger landing gear without wheel pants.*

Built by the thousands; a largely wood spar and plywood exterior basic trainer flown by nearly a million WWII student pilots. Faster and sturdier than most biplanes of that era. When fitted with radial engines, known as the PT-23—a much less common type than the PT-19. Greenhouse canopy supplied on Canadian Air Force versions (the Cornell) and on the few civilian models, designated M62. All were remarkably durable (although the wood construction has created problems after the passage of nearly 50 years) and regarded as forgiving and easy to fly.

Consolidated Vultee Valiant, BT-13, BT-15, SNV-1

Length: 28'7" (8.65 m)   *Wingspan:* 42' (12.8 m)   *Cruising speed:* 170 mph (274 km/h)

Quite rare, although 10,000 built through WWII. An odd combination: *fully enclosed radial engine and large fixed tail-dragging gear* (the somewhat similar T-6 is a retractable tail dragger, page 47). *Tall, narrow tail fin.*

Vultee developed the basic trainer BT-13 before merging with Consolidated and built them through WWII; they were still in military service as late as 1950. Known to a generation of pilots as "the Vibrator"—more a reference to what it did to airport windows than what it did to the pilots. Of the thousands that went on the war surplus market, most were cannibalized—the Valiant's Wasp Junior radial engine fit the Stearman Kaydet, a popular sportster and crop duster.

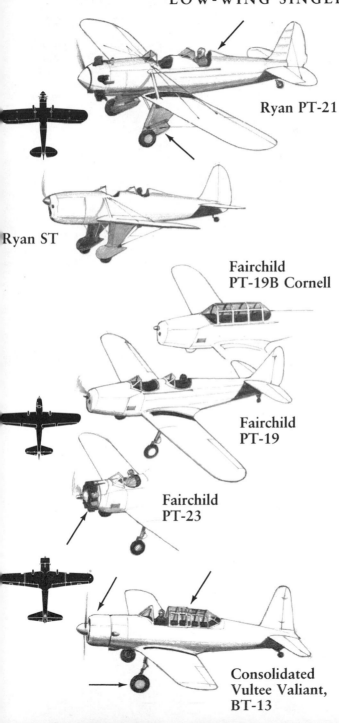

LOW-WING SINGLES

Ryan PT-21

Ryan ST

Fairchild
PT-19B Cornell

Fairchild
PT-19

Fairchild
PT-23

Consolidated
Vultee Valiant,
BT-13

de Havilland DHC1 Chipmunk

Length: 25'5" (7.75 m)   *Wingspan:* 34'4" (10.46 m)   *Cruising speed:* 124 mph (200 km/h)

Rare in the U.S., more common in Canada. *Unbraced low wing; fixed tail-dragging gear.* Compared to the Fairchild PT-19 Cornell, the Chipmunk has a *short, two-pane greenhouse canopy* that sits much farther back than the Fairchild's. A large air intake sits under the propeller spinner and is offset sharply to the port side of the aircraft.

Created in Canada to replace the biplane DH82 Tiger Moth as a primary trainer, the Chipmunk was built from 1946 to 1953 in Canada and Great Britain. It is the most antique looking of all the post–WWII all-metal construction aircraft. If you have a chance to see one near a Gipsy Moth or a Tiger Moth, note the similarity in the slimness of the fuselage and the shape of the engine cowling— the Chipmunk is very much a one-winged Moth.

Varga Kachina

Length: 21'2" (6.45 m)   *Wingspan:* 30' (9.14 m)   *Cruising speed:* 127 mph (204 km/h)

A *small, low-wing single,* of modern all-metal construction, but with an *old-fashioned-looking "fighter" cockpit canopy* that covers tandem seating; *near constant-chord* (width) *wings with rounded tips; upright tail fin.*

A design created in wood and fabric construction by William Morrisey, a Douglas test pilot, after WWII. Known then as the Morrisey Nifty. Redesigned in all metal in the 1960s. Many sold with *tail-dragging* gear, to appeal to the owner who wants to increase the illusion that he's flying a WWII fighter plane. Built standard with dual controls; a popular sport and training aircraft, particularly for the weekend rental market.

Gulfstream American Yankee, T-Cat, Lynx, AA-1, AA-5

Length: 19'3" (5.86 m)   *Wingspan:* 24'5" (7.45 m)   *Cruising speed:* 135 mph (217 km/h)

A series of fairly common *unbraced low-wing, fixed tricycle gear two-seaters.* The *constant-chord* (width) *wings have a strong dihedral, and small fillet-fairings* on both edges at the wing root; *bubble canopy* plus *small side window.*

Created by noted small-plane designer Jim Bede using modern honeycomb and metal-to-metal bonded construction. Built by Bede Aviation in 1972; then American Aviation; then by Grumman American; finally by Gulfstream American, until 1978. The model illustrated is the Lynx, with wheel pants. There were models built with standard dual controls for primary training. Lower drawing of four-place Gulfstream American Cheetah, a stretched Lynx with a conventional cockpit canopy.

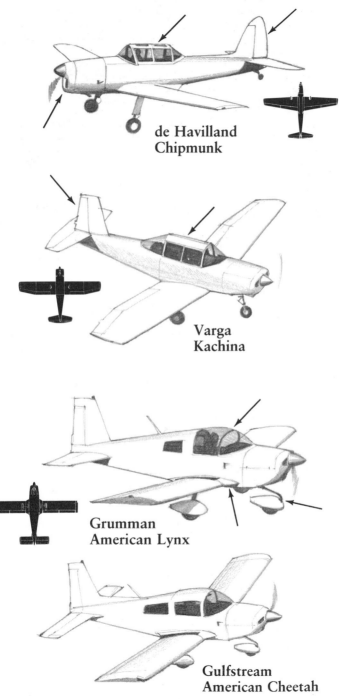

LOW-WING SINGLES

de Havilland
Chipmunk

Varga
Kachina

Grumman
American Lynx

Gulfstream
American Cheetah

Beech Skipper 77

Length: 24' (7.32 m)   *Wingspan:* 30' (9.14 m)   *Cruising speed:* 112 mph (180 km/h)

Increasingly common fixed-gear trainer. Compare with Piper Tomahawk before deciding. Skipper has *Hershey-bar wing* (with fillet-fairing to leading edge) *and tail plane, true T-tail; trapezoidal side window in each door;* shorter and wider wings than the Piper Tomahawk. Skipper *main landing gear is spraddle-legged,* leaning back and out, giving the plane a very wide stance on the runway.

In use by 1979, a year after the competitive Tomahawk. The primary trainer for company-franchised Beech Aero Centers. Originally planned as a conventional-tail aircraft and so flown as a prototype in 1978; the T-tail was apparently triggered by the success of the Tomahawk in 1978.

Piper PA38 Tomahawk

Length: 23'1" (7.03 m)   *Wingspan:* 34' (10.36 m)   *Cruising speed:* 114 mph (183 km/h)

Very common trainer. *Pure Hershey-bar wing and tail plane without any fillets or fairings.* Wing is visibly longer and slimmer than on comparable Beech Skipper; *not quite a T-tail* (a cross-tail); *rectangular window in each door.*

Piper's very successful entrant into the modern trainer market, more than 1000 ordered in the first year (1978). Achieves the same wide stance as the Tomahawk (for better runway control) but without the spraddle-legged look. Tomahawk's 4-foot 9-inch wheelbase was achieved by wing-mounting the main gear; Skipper's 5-foot 2-inch wheelbase requires longer wheel struts since it arises at the root of the wing and fuselage.

Ercoupe (Alon Aircoupe, Mooney M10 Cadet)

Length: 20'9" (6.32 m)   *Wingspan:* 30' (9.14 m)   *Cruising speed:* 110 mph (177 km/h)

Increasingly rare. *Distinctive twin fin tail* is unique on single-engine aircraft; *strong dihedral in constant-chord* (width) *wings; rounded wing tips.*

Designed and first built just before WWII, the Ercoupe was intended as a plane for Sunday drivers, and survived until 1970 (Mooney M10 Cadet). Used a conventional steering wheel that moved the ailerons and rudder simultaneously for turning; angle of climb and descent governed normally, by pushing or pulling on the "steering column" stick. It's designed to be spin and stall proof, if not idiot proof. Ercoupe also introduced the tricycle landing gear to the private pilot, making it astonishingly easy to fly off the runway. The lack of foot pedals also made flying accessible to many handicapped pilots. (It looked so easy that the author's father talked of buying one—until the author's mother overheard him.)

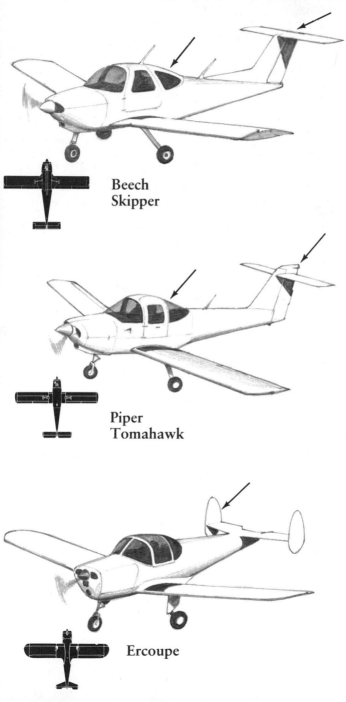

LOW-WING SINGLES

Beech
Skipper

Piper
Tomahawk

Ercoupe

Beech Sierra (retractable),
Sundowner, Sport, Musketeer

Length: 25'9" (7.85 m) *Wingspan:* 32'9" (9.98 m) *Cruising speed:* 158 mph (254 km/h)

All models quite common. Top drawing: Sierra. *Retractable gear folds outward; wheels remain visible under wing; long, thin, rectangular tail plane; perfectly rectangular wings enter fuselage without any fairing.* A distinct field mark, when you have other similarly sized airplanes to compare with it, is the *high cockpit ceiling.* All two-window versions seat three; those with three or four side windows seat five, including the pilot.

Developed in 1969 as a retractable-gear Musketeer; marketed since 1971 as the Sierra. Early versions were regarded as slow and klutzy. Major changes included increased engine power (from 170 to 200 hp) and aerodynamic fairings underwing to shield the retracted wheels—the so-called speed bumps. Still not a high-performance aircraft, but it's roomy inside, with unusually good pilot visibility.

Middle drawing: Musketeer II. No longer manufactured. Wings and tail surfaces are identical to Sierra, but with fixed gear. Oldest models of Musketeer have two side windows.

Bottom drawing: Sundowner. In production. Distinguish from other fixed-gear Musketeer types by the larger side windows (note rear window in particular) and the longer propeller spinner and slightly more streamlined engine cowling. A two-window version, with same large spinner and streamlined cowling, is the Sport.

Aerospatiale (SOCATA) Rallye

Length: 23'9" (7.24 m) *Wingspan:* 31'6" (9.61 m) *Cruising speed:* 108 mph (174 km/h)

A *low-wing with fixed tricycle gear; large one-piece side window on glass canopy; wing and tail plane are constant chord* (width). When in view, note the substantial *bullet-shaped "close-out" fairing* at the tail end of the fuselage.

A variable series of small planes with two-, three-, and four-seat versions, built in France since 1958. Various names for different models—Sport, Tourisme, Club, and Minerva. It's been imported into the U.S. and Canada since 1974; the most common model is the 225-horsepower Minerva. The Hershey-bar wing and tail plane resembles certain Piper models, and, curiously, Piper was the U.S. importer in the 1970s.

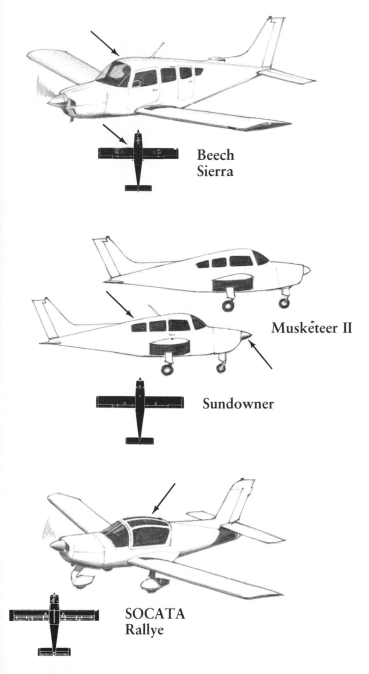

Beech
Sierra

Musketeer II

Sundowner

SOCATA
Rallye

Piper PA28-180R Cherokee Arrow, Arrow II, Arrow III

Length: 24'2" (7.37 m) *Wingspan:* 32' (9.75 m) *Cruising speed:* 162 mph (261 km/h)

Less common than the nonretractable Cherokee series. *Identical to the fixed-gear Cherokees* (see the Piper PA28 Cherokee and Cherokee Warrior field notes, below). For simplicity's sake: The Arrow II (illustrated) has three side windows and constant-chord wings; a two-window Arrow is a I. The Arrow III has the new, tapered Piper wing and is identical to the Cherokee Warrior II with tapered wings, except for its retractable gear. There are a few Arrow IIIs with turbocharged engines (see bottom sketch next to Arrow IV, page 33, showing the turbocharger air scoop). On the flight line with wheels down, an Arrow is a *Cherokee without wheel pants.* On the air traffic controller's radio, they're all just plain Cherokees.

Piper PA28 Cherokee 140, 150, 160

Length: 23'3" (7.08 m) *Wingspan:* 30' (9.14 m) *Cruising speed:* with 180-horsepower engine, 130 mph (209 km/h)

Common. *Small four-seater, candy-bar wing, fixed tricycle gear with wheel pants.*

Introduced in 1961, superseded by the Cherokee Warrior in 1974, when it received the multi-angled "new Piper" wing. Engines built with 140 to 235 horsepower. The plane was eventually designated Charger. When stretched to hold six, it became the Cherokee SIX (page 32). The 150-horsepower version, designated Flite-Liner, was a popular club plane and trainer in the 1970s. The original Cherokee introduced considerable use of simple curves and fiberglass and plastic construction to the small-plane market.

Piper PA28 Cherokee Warrior, Warrior II

Length: 23'9" (7.25 m) *Wingspan:* 35' (10.67 m) *Cruising speed:* 135 mph (217 km/h)

Common. *Fixed tricycle gear;* always with wheel pants; note *streamlining on main wheel gear, compared to nose; dihedral in wing, none in tail; three side windows.* Wing is of complicated geometry: leaves fuselage *with fairing to leading edge; short equal-span section; leading and trailing edges taper to tip at unequal angles. Tail plane a pure Hershey-bar rectangle.*

Flown since 1974, the first Piper to abandon their trademark of constant-chord (width) wing plans. Sold under various names with slight differences, including engine horsepower: Cherokee Warrior, renamed Warrior II (160 hp), Dakota (235 hp), Archer II (180 hp). All versions seat four, including the pilot.

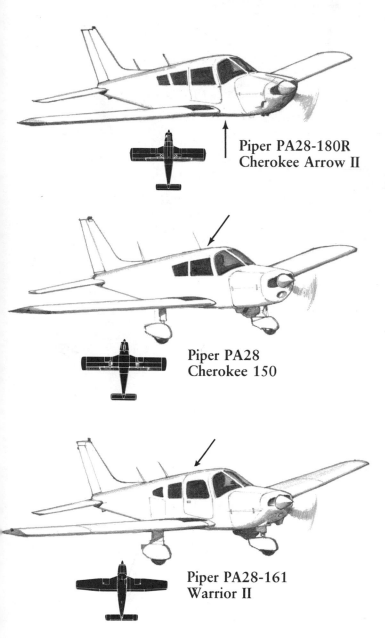

Piper PA28-180R
Cherokee Arrow II

Piper PA28
Cherokee 150

Piper PA28-161
Warrior II

Piper PA32 Cherokee SIX, PA32R-300 Lance, PA32RT-300 Lance II

Length: 27'9" (8.45 m) *Wingspan:* 32'9" (9.95 m) *Cruising speed:* 158 mph (254 km/h)

A common, *large, fixed-gear airplane.* Typical early Piper wing—a Hershey-bar rectangle with fairing to leading edge; *an oversized Cherokee with four side windows.* The earliest models had four squared windows, not the variable geometrical shapes seen in the sketch. A retractable Cherokee SIX, with Hershey-bar wings, is a Lance, of which a few models had T-tails (upper sketch).

Carrying six, including the pilot, for many years (1964–1979) it was Piper's largest single-engine and the largest fixed-gear single in the private aviation field. When equipped with an optional 300-horsepower engine, it's suitable for use on skis or floats. Occasionally used as an air ambulance or short-haul freighter; then equipped with a single large door at the rear of the cabin that folds up. Last produced in 1979, when Piper replaced it with the non-retractable PA32 Saratoga, using the longer, tapered, "new Piper" wing plan.

Piper PA32R-301 Saratoga

Length: 28'4" (8.64 m) *Wingspan:* 36'2" (11.02 m) *Cruising speed:* 162 mph (261 km/h)

What we have here is *a Cherokee SIX with the new, tapered Piper wing.* If you can't get a look at the wing, call it a Cherokee.

The Saratoga is a six-passenger addition, usually sold with retractable gear, many with turbocharged engines (see sketch under main drawing). The Saratoga basically replaced the Cherokee SIX and the T-tailed Lance; it has been in production since 1979. The name change signifies mostly the wing change, plus more horsepower.

Piper PA28RT Arrow IV

Length: 27' (8.23 m) *Wingspan:* 35'5" (10.80 m) *Cruising speed:* 165 mph (265 km/h)

Not especially common. What we have here is *a Cherokee Warrior II with a T-tail.* Has the *tapered wings of the Warrior series* (page 30). A much larger plane than the little T-tailed Beech Skipper; fully retractable gear.

If there was ever any proof that the T-tail had some sales advantages, as opposed to utilitarian purpose, it was sticking one on the old reliable Cherokee Warrior II/Archer airframes in 1977. The T-tail Arrow IV comes in conventional and turbocharged models, as does the Arrow III (see bottom sketch showing air intake).

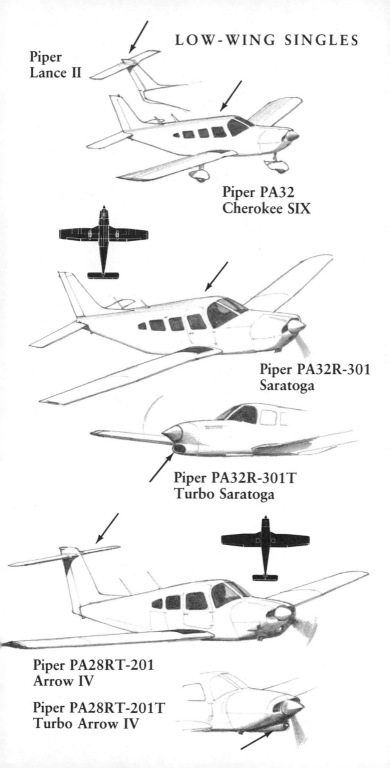

LOW-WING SINGLES

Piper
Lance II

Piper PA32
Cherokee SIX

Piper PA32R-301
Saratoga

Piper PA32R-301T
Turbo Saratoga

Piper PA28RT-201
Arrow IV

Piper PA28RT-201T
Turbo Arrow IV

Beechcraft Bonanza 35, 33

Length: 26'5" (8.05 m)   *Wingspan:* 33'6" (10.21 m)   *Cruising speed:* 190 mph (306 km/h)

Anything with a *V-tail* is a Bonanza 35. Confusion is generated by two conventional-tail aircraft, the Bonanza 36 (next entry) and the Bonanza 33, which is identical to the Bonanza 35 except that it has a conventional tail. (See the Bonanza 36 entry for details.)

Built from 1947 to date, more than 10,000 are flying in North America. About 1200 were built with only two side windows, before 1961; however, some owners have added the third side window to their own pre-1961 aircraft. It comes with a variety of engines, including turbocharging. Early models had a smaller tail surface, less steeply angled, but after-market modifications have been made to most of those. Of all-metal construction since its inception.

Beechcraft Bonanza 36

Length: 27'6" (8.38 m)   *Wingspan:* 33'6" (10.21 m)   *Cruising speed:* 188 mph (302 km/h)

Commonest of the large, single-engine, retractable-gear planes. *Fairing from fuselage to wing's leading edge; four side windows; large doors on starboard side.* If you take the Beech 35, above, and put a Beech 36 conventional tail on it, you have the Beech Bonanza 33 (once known as the Debonair).

Built since 1968, it seats six, including the pilot; for many years, the only six-passenger, retractable-gear single. Turbocharged model (illustrated) shows intake and cooling louvers on engine cowling. The smaller Debonair/Bonanza 33 has three side windows and seats four, including the pilot. Since 1982, the turbocharged model has a 37-foot 6-inch (11.43-m) wingspan.

North American Rockwell Commander 111, 112, 114

Length: 25' (7.62 m)   *Wingspan:* 32'11" (10.04 m)   *Cruising speed:* 157 mph (253 km/h)

Not common. Best field mark for this low-wing single is the *tail plane, mounted midway up the tail fin.* Overhead, the *wing leading edge is straight, at right angles to the centerline,* except for the noticeable fairing from fuselage to leading edge; strong (7-degree) dihedral in wing, none in tail plane; a wide, chubby look to the cabin area.

Built since 1971, it's a high-performance, four-seat single. The unusual tail design caused some difficulty at first, including the loss of a prototype, and the requirement to redesign the rear fuselage and tail assembly. The interior cabin space is unusually wide for a four-passenger single and gives the aircraft its look of being bulky forward and over the wing.

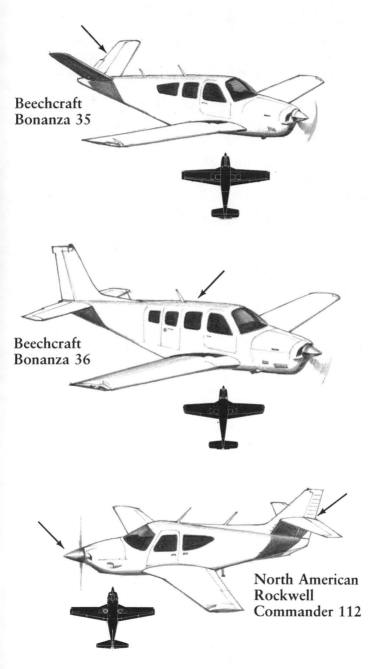

Beechcraft
Bonanza 35

Beechcraft
Bonanza 36

North American
Rockwell
Commander 112

Piper PA46 Malibu

Length: 28'4" (8.63 m)   *Wingspan:* 43' (13.11 m)   *Cruising speed:* estimated, 230 mph (370 km/h)

New in 1983. Marked by *a heavy look to the fuselage; long, thin wings.*

The Malibu, which is turbocharged and pressurized, can operate to 25,000 feet. The cabin is unusually large for a single (4 feet by 4 feet, interior dimensions) and does not taper from the forward to the rear seats—note the field mark of a rotund fuselage. The wing design is quite unusual for a commercial aircraft: The ratio of wing length to width (chord) is 11 to 1 (most business-style aircraft ratios are about 7 to 1). It seats six, including the crew.

Beechcraft Lightning 38P

Length: 29'10" (9.09 m)   *Wingspan:* 37'10" (11.53 m)   *Cruising speed:* 250 mph (402 km/h)

New to the market in 1984. The best field mark will be the unusual sound of *turbopropeller whine* in a single-engine plane; *two large exhausts below engine; airscoop under propeller spinner, not unlike a P-51's; very long-nosed.*

Beech has the first turboprop single intended for the business market. (Their T-34 Navy trainer is a small aerobatic plane.) The fuselage and tail are identical to the twin-engine Beech Baron; the wing, except without engines, is also. The plane will be pressurized, with a ceiling of approximately 25,000 feet.

Piper PA24 Comanche

Length: 25' (7.62 m)   *Wingspan:* 36' (10.98 m)   *Cruising speed:* 182 mph (293 km/h)

Chunky fuselage; commonly, two side windows, last models had three; retractable gear is visible, tucked in against fuselage; Beech Bonanza–type wing, fairing to a straight leading edge, tapered trailing edge.

Piper's first low-wing was also its first retractable. The wing appears to be a Beech borrow, but is in fact a U.S. government design—several thousand were built before production ended in 1972. For the last few years, the plane stretched the cabin to seat five or six and added the third window, at which point Piper shifted to the Arrow series (page 30) as the standard six-passenger retractable.

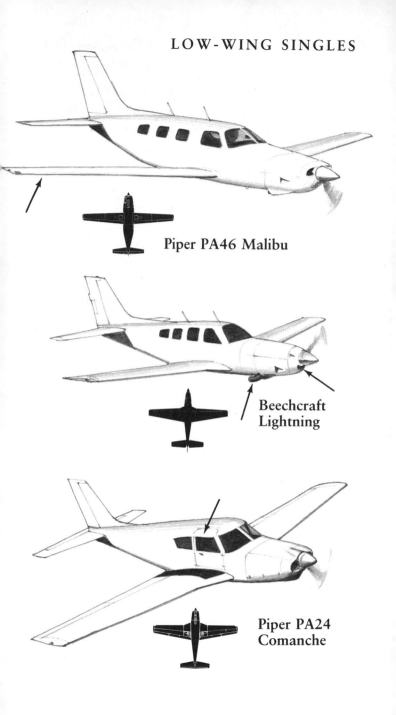

Piper PA46 Malibu

Beechcraft
Lightning

Piper PA24
Comanche

Mooney Aircraft Corporation (briefly, Aerostar)

A series of four-place, tricycle-gear aircraft with common field marks. *All leading edges—wing, tail fin, and tail plane—are straight lines, at right angles to the centerline of the airplane. All trailing surfaces angle forward;* gives the planes the image of leaning forward into the air. *Compare the small, tail-dragging Mooney Mite* (page 44).

Mooney 201 (top drawing), 231

Length: 24'8" (7.52 m) *Wingspan:* 36'1" (11 m) *Cruising speed:* 167 mph (269 km/h)

One of the models currently being built. Difficult to separate from other Mooneys, but has *longer, rectangular side windows* compared to the M20 Chapparal types (center drawing).

The 231 is identical to the Mooney 201, except with turbo-charged engine in *slightly longer (9-inch) engine cowling.*

Mooney M20 Chapparal

Length: 23'2" (7.06 m) *Wingspan:* 35' (10.67 m) *Cruising speed:* 172 mph (277 km/h)

A series of very similar Mooneys, various engines and names, including Executive 21, Chapparal, and Super 21. There are some aerodynamically important streamlining details, but none really visible. The most recent version, the Ranger (not illustrated), has fully covered wheel wells and lacks the dorsal fin fairing to the tail fin. All *windows a bit smaller than on the Mooney 201, 231.*

When Mooney was owned by Butler Aviation (1969–1972) production airplanes (Super 21, Executive, and Ranger) carried the odd buttonhook tail design (see sketch next to the Chapparal drawing).

Mooney M22 Mustang

Length: 26'10" (8.18 m) *Wingspan:* 35' (10.67 m) *Cruising speed:* 214 mph (344 km/h)

Rare, built only from 1967 to 1969. *Pressurized,* which shows in the window design; *four small side windows—three square, trailing window round.* A very high performance single, with a 24,000-foot operating ceiling.

Mooney M20D Master, and Mark 21

Length: 23'2" (7.06 m) *Wingspan:* 35' (10.67 m) *Cruising speeds:* 130–150 mph (209–241 km/h)

The original production all-metal Mooneys. The Mooney M20D Master has *fixed tricycle gear, but lacks typical dorsal fin fairing to tail.* The Mooney Master, with retractable gear, grew up into the Mooney Ranger.

The Mooney M20C (last drawing), with retractable gear, would grow into the Mark 21 and be the parent of the Chapparal, Mark 201, and Mark 231 Mooneys. It has the dorsal fin. Both these early four-place Mooneys show a *distinct air-intake "chin"* below the propeller spinner.

LOW-WING SINGLES

Mooney 201

Mooney 231

Aerostar

Mooney M20
Chapparal

Mooney M22
Mustang

Mooney M20D
Master

Mooney M20C

Navion Rangemaster

Length: 27'6" (8.38 m)   *Wingspan:* 34'9" (10.59 m)   *Cruising speed:* 290 mph (467 km/h)

A rare, odd bird: a *low-wing single with tip-tanks.* It's essentially similar in wing and tail configuration to the Ryan Navion, but with a built-up five-passenger cabin and automobile-type door on the port side of the aircraft.

A Texas aircraft parts manufacturer picked up the old Ryan Navion design, spare parts, and tools to manufacture the Rangemaster—all quite similar except for the cabin, and supplied with a variety of engines. Like the prototype, it comes standard with dual controls.

Ryan Navion (L-17), North American Aviation Navion

Length: 27'8" (8.43 m)   *Wingspan:* 33'5" (10.18 m)   *Cruising speed:* 155 mph (249 km/h)

Rare. A low-wing single with a *bulbous cockpit canopy and slender rear fuselage. Nose wheel is visible* when tricycle gear is retracted. Could easily be confused with the even rarer Aero Commander 200 (next entry): *Navion's rear side window tapers sharply; two-piece windshield with noticeable center strip,* whereas the Aero Commander has a much larger rear window that sweeps up, and a one-piece windshield.

Manufactured in the late 1940s through 1951, it seats four, including the pilot. Ryan built hundreds of low-wing trainers during WWII, but purchased the Navion design from North American. Came standard with dual controls and a bench seat for two more passengers. Canopy slides back for access to cabin. Ryan added landing gear doors and personal comfort items to the basic North American design.

Aero Commander 200 (Meyers 200)

Length: 24'4" (7.42 m)   *Wingspan:* 30'6" (9.29 m)   *Cruising speed:* 215 mph (346 km/h)

Quite rare. A small *retractable tricycle gear,* distinguished by a *high cabin canopy,* automobile-type door on starboard side of the cabin. *Appearance is short-winged, slim-fuselaged,* aft of *bulbous canopy.* Could be confused with the Ryan Navion.

Aero Commander took over the Meyers 200, buying a design that put them in the high-performance, four-seat, retractable market in 1965. Very few Meyers 200s and not many more (perhaps 100) Aero Commander 200s were built from 1965 to 1967. Built with various engines, including one type with a turboprop, the Interceptor 400, with cruising speeds near 300 mph. More fun to fly than practical.

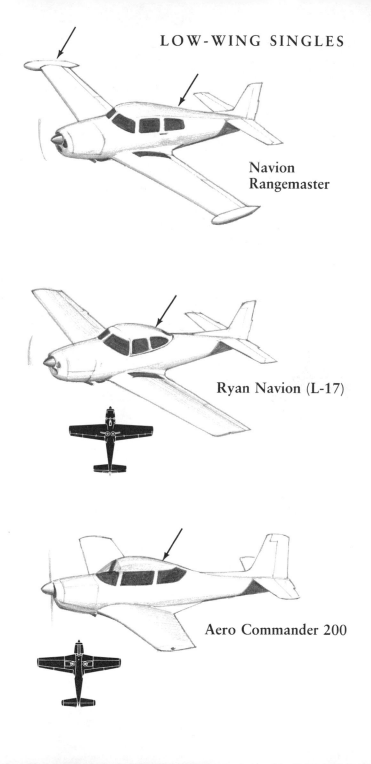

LOW-WING SINGLES

Navion Rangemaster

Ryan Navion (L-17)

Aero Commander 200

Temco (Globe) Swift 125

Length: 20'11" (6.38 m)   *Wingspan:* 29'4" (8.94 m)   *Cruising speed:* 140 mph (225 km/h)

Rare. A *small retractable, low-wing;* cockpit and windows varied, not good field marks; *strong (8-degree) dihedral in tail plane and wings*—very unusual in small singles and a distinct field mark at any altitude or attitude. Close at hand, a *unique engine grill,* like something from a 1950s General Motors automobile.

A few hundred of these 1945–1951 airplanes survive. They came standard with dual controls, some with all-Plexiglas canopy, some with enclosed cabin. Along with the Mooney Mite, one of the first post–WWII airplanes to take advantage of the wind-tunnel-tested wing designs of the National Advisory Committee on Aeronautics (NACA), precursor of NASA. Many fly today with much more powerful engines than the original 125 horsepower.

Bellanca Viking (and Cruisemaster 14193C)

Length: 26'4" (8.02 m)   *Wingspan:* 34'2" (10.41 m)   *Cruising speed:* 185 mph (298 km/h)

A small low-wing; *large strongly swept tail fin; strut under tail planes; dihedral in wing, none in tail plane; wraparound windshield; two large side windows; nose wheel does not retract fully, main gear carried in underwing fairings.*

Bellanca essentially took the Cruisemaster (next entry), added a tricycle gear, and dropped the outboard fins on the tail planes to make the Cruisemaster 14193. The swept tail fin was added in 1958, the name changed to Viking in 1966. No longer manufactured, although efforts are occasionally made to reintroduce it. Constructed of fabric over plywood and tubing.

Bellanca Cruisemaster, Cruiseair

Cruisemaster specifications: *Length:* 22'11" (7 m)   *Wingspan:* 34'2" (10.41 m)   *Cruising speed:* 180 mph (290 km/h)

Rare. *A stubby low-wing tail-dragger; main gear remains exposed when retracted; triple-tailed; central tail fin much larger than outboard fins; wire braces on tail plane; two side windows.*

About 100 Cruisemasters and a few hundred very similar Cruiseairs (smaller engines) were built from 1946 to 1958. Plane combined relatively high operating speeds with low landing speeds and a stall speed of about 50 mph. Highly regarded for sport use. Seats three, including the pilot. Construction is fabric over plywood.

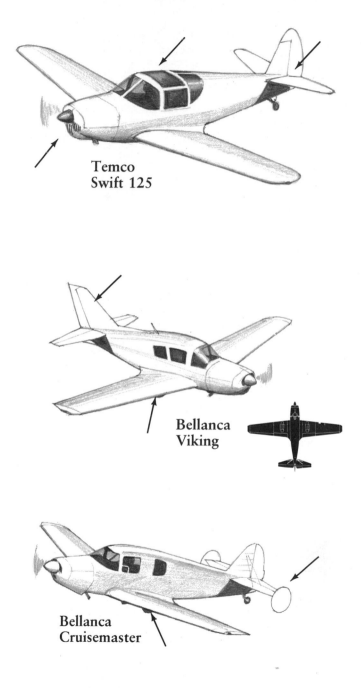

Temco
Swift 125

Bellanca
Viking

Bellanca
Cruisemaster

Mooney M18 Mite

Length: 18' (5.48 m) *Wingspan:* 26'10" (8.20 m) *Cruising speed:* 80 mph (129 km/h)

Rare. A classic Mooney design. Though *tiny, a one-seater,* it has same wing and tail surface pattern as the four-seat Mooneys—*leading edges of wing and tail surfaces are a straight line at right angles to the centerline of the fuselage.*

Built from 1947 to 1954, the Mooney Mite was a favorite sport plane for ex–fighter pilots—inexpensive to own, cheap to fly—but it did not answer the needs of the family-oriented pilot. Originally designed to use the old Crosley automobile engine, the last models (M18) had a regulation 65-horsepower aircraft engine. Still available in kit form. The first post–WWII civilian aircraft to use a NACA wing design.

Culver LCA Cadet

Length: 17'8" (5.3 m) *Wingspan:* 26'11" (8.1 m) *Cruising speed:* 120 mph (193 km/h)

Rare. A *very small low-wing retractable;* dihedral in wings, none in tail plane. Overhead, there is a *semi-elliptical curve to both edges of wings and tail plane.* Plane has a distinct sculptured look to it, with smooth curves everywhere, as though carved from a bar of soap. Structure mainly wood, with early fiberglass reinforcement and fuselage skin.

Built from 1939 through WWII, with a few bench-built copies as late as 1960. Final design was by Al Mooney, creator of the Mooney line of aircraft; the fastest and nimblest of pre–WWII private aircraft. Used during the war as radio-controlled target drone, and pilot-flown as "camera-gun" target for training Air Force gunners and pilots. So acrobatic, it was a satisfactory imitation of the hottest enemy fighter planes. It is one of the curiosities of life that Al Mooney was never brought in to design U.S. fighter planes.

North American T-28 Trojan

Length: 32' (9.76 m) *Wingspan:* 40'1" (12.23 m) *Cruising speed:* 190 mph (306 km/h)

Not common. In civilian colors; *fat engine cowling* houses large radial engine; *long, high, Plexiglas canopy* sits atop tandem-seating dual controls; *tall, sharply angular tail fin. Plane is heavy, chunky.*

In the 1950s and 1960s, the common U.S. armed forces basic trainer sank like a rock with engine failure. It was adapted, like many trainers, to a counterinsurgency role with underwing bomb and rocket mounts. A counterinsurgency role usually implies enough power to carry bombs, but only against a lightly defended target. There have been a few civilian conversions with cabins replacing the cockpit/canopy, but the general configuration is unchanged. In use in Florida as primary aircraft carrier trainer by U.S. Navy.

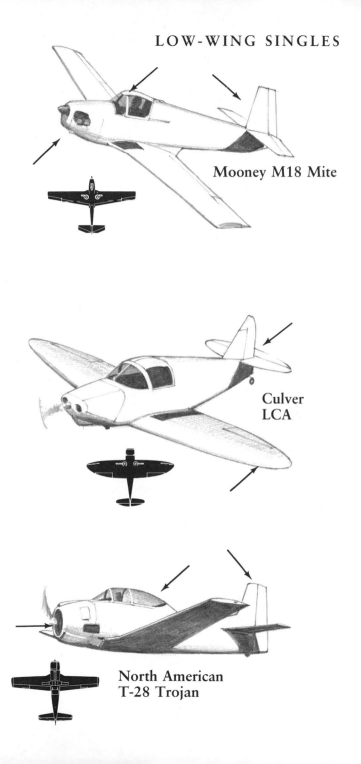

LOW-WING SINGLES

Mooney M18 Mite

Culver
LCA

North American
T-28 Trojan

North American T-6 Texan, Harvard II

Length: 29'6" (8.99 m)   *Wingspan:* 42' (12.80 m)   *Cruising speed:* 218 mph (351 km/h)

A fairly common relic of WWII. *Long greenhouse canopy* over tandem dual controls; *dihedral in wing begins a few feet out from fuselage* (a "reverse gull-wing," as in Corsair). Close at hand or overhead, note the *rounded bump where the leading edge of the wing meets the fuselage;* this is a fairing to hold the retracted main gear wheels. *Tail fin is quite triangular.*

Built before 1941 and in service through the Korean conflict, the Texan, purchased as military surplus, was a popular sport plane for veteran pilots. More often seen parked than in the air. Attention-attracting noise, when flying. More than 15,000 produced between 1941 and 1951. Overhead, the wing is typical of pre–WWII design: nearly straight trailing edge, tapering leading edge—like a single-engine DC3.

Beech T-34A, B Mentor

Length: 25'10" (7.80 m)   *Wingspan:* 32'10" (10 m)   *Cruising speed:* 160 mph (257 km/h)

Not common. Large *greenhouse canopy* over tandem dual-control cockpit; *large, slablike, upright tail fin.* The clear "trainer look" combined with a nonradial engine separates the Mentor from the Texan and the Trojan.

In civilian hands, a popular low-wing aerobatic aircraft. In military service from 1954 to 1960 as a common USAF and Navy basic trainer, replacing the T-6 Trojan. Flown by the Navy only from 1960 to 1980. The Air Force moved to all-through jet training during the years from 1960 to 1964, when most of the civilian-owned Mentors came on the market. Curiously, after all-through jet training was deemed a failure by the Air Force, it turned to Cessna's 172 Skyhawk (page 76), a slow, high-wing prop plane, for the first 30 hours of training, designating it the T-41 Mescalero.

Grumman TBF-1 (TBM-1) Avenger, "Borate Bomber"

Length: 40' (12.2 m)   *Wingspan:* 54'2" (16.5 m)   *Cruising speed:* 240 mph (386 km/h)

A *very rare, large, single-engine* military aircraft. *Original greenhouse cockpit canopy usually modified, but not in any standard manner; lower fuselage (bomb bay) steps up to tail section; square-cut tail surfaces.*

Now restricted to museums, except for a few that are flying, particularly in Canada, as aerial forest-fire fighters, dropping "borated" or otherwise treated water on fires. Gawky, ungainly, but a fairly successful torpedo bomber. Holds a crew of three: the pilot, bombardier/navigator, and gunner. The TBM-1 was identical, manufactured by General Motors under license from Grumman.

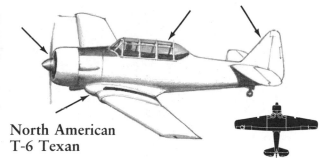

North American
T-6 Texan

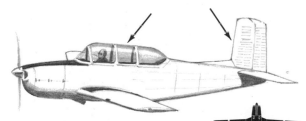

Beech
T-34 Mentor

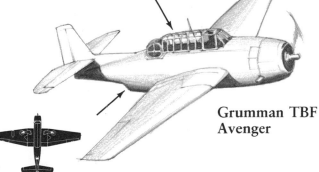

Grumman TBF
Avenger

Chance Vought F-4U Corsair

Length: 33'8" (10.26 m)   *Wingspan:* 41' (12.49 m)   *Cruising speed:* 350 mph (563 km/h)

Unmistakable. *A large, noisy, radial-engine warship* with a one-man cockpit set halfway back on the fuselage. *Wings drop down from fuselage, then show sharp dihedral to tip: "reverse gull-wing."* May be seen in hangars with the wings folded up.

More than 12,000 F-4Us were produced through WWII; saw most service in 1944 and 1945. One of the most powerful (2000–3000 horsepower, six .50-caliber machine guns, plus two tons of bombs or rockets) fighter-bombers ever built. Nicknamed "Whistling Death" by Japanese pilots. The subject of the only literary poem ever written about a U.S. warplane, "Ode to an F4U Fighter" by Yvor Winters.

North American P-51 Mustang

Length: 32'3" (9.83 m)   *Wingspan:* 37' (11.28 m)   *Cruising speed:* 390 mph (628 km/h)

Rare. Most often seen at air shows. *Long, slim nose with massive propeller spinner.* From the side or below, note that the *radiator air intake* for the liquid-cooled engine is *set well back under the cockpit* (visible in lower sketch). Tail arrangement is unusual; *tail planes set very high and well forward* (to clear the full-length rudder on the tail fin).

Developed by North American in 1940 to meet a British specification for a long-range fighter-escort for British bombers that would operate over Europe from bases in England. Top drawing shows the most common P-51D, with a bubble canopy for good vision to the rear. Bottom sketch shows the turtleback style of the P-51A-C types. The Cavalier Aircraft Company has built modern P-51-Ds with *tip-tanks* to be used as counterinsurgency planes by U.S. allies. This design was acquired by Piper Aircraft, which continued to develop the aircraft as the "Enforcer" until 1984. Counterinsurgency aircraft, as we have noted, are best defined as easily maintained fighter-bombers for use against lightly defended persons and dwellings.

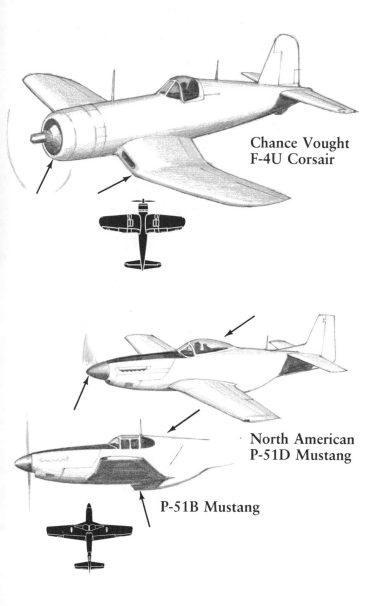

Chance Vought
F-4U Corsair

North American
P-51D Mustang

P-51B Mustang

de Havilland (Canada) DHC3 Otter

Length: 41'10" (12.80 m)   *Wingspan:* 58' (17.69 m)   *Cruising speed:* 121 mph (195 km/h)

Fairly common in the Far West, Alaska, and Canada. *Massive single-braced high-wing tail-dragger, with huge radial engine;* nearly two-thirds the size of a DC3. If you've never seen a de Havilland Beaver or Otter before, note the passenger windows —Otters show six rectangular side windows behind a cockpit window configuration that's similar to the much smaller Beaver.

Built from 1952 to 1967, this late design carries the most massive, antique appearing tail assembly of any post–WWII aircraft. Essentially an upscaled Beaver (the design project was called "King Beaver"), it carries up to ten passengers. Single 600-horsepower radial engine proved quite reliable, even in the Arctic. Not uncommon on floats, particularly with small Alaskan and Canadian air-taxi operators.

de Havilland (Canada) DHC2 Beaver, U-6

Length: 30'4" (9.24 m)   *Wingspan:* 48' (14.64 m)   *Cruising speed:* with radial, 135 mph (217 km/h); with turboprop, 157 mph (253 km/h)

A common float plane; less common elsewhere. Massive *single-braced high wing,* much more common with radial engine (top drawing). Land versions with *fixed one-rung ladder.* Factory-standard *float planes with multirunged ladder and curved ventral finlet under tail fin. Trapezoidal passenger window with trailing "porthole" window* is typical on all models.

Built from 1948 to 1969; seats up to eight, including the pilot. All-metal construction. Numbers of them have crashed and been totally rebuilt. The less common turboprop (built between 1964 and 1969) also introduced the swept tail fin of modern design, as it did a fuselage-lengthening that put the cabin forward of the wing (bottom sketch).

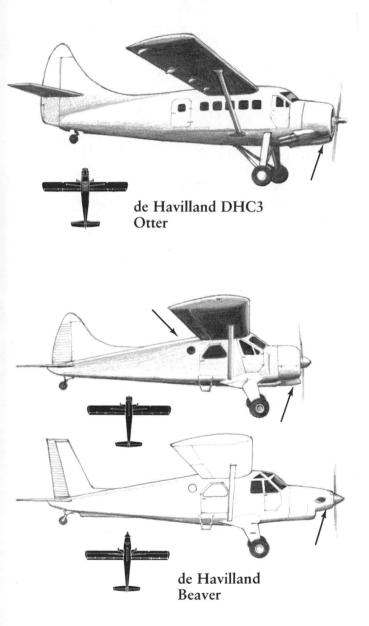

de Havilland DHC3
Otter

de Havilland
Beaver

Cessna 190/195 Businessliner

Length: 27'1" (8.26 m)   *Wingspan:* 36'2" (11 m)   *Cruising speed:*
160 mph (257 km/h)

Not common. A unique combination of *a tail-dragger with
skinny spring-steel wheel struts; big radial engine in a bumpy cowling; all-metal skin; and unbraced high wing.* Nothing else puts all
that together.

A four-place luxury plane built from 1947 to 1954, the largest,
fastest, roomiest, and easily the most expensive of the early postwar private planes. Model numbers refer to type of engine. A factory-standard float plane incorporates a three-finned tail, instead of
the usual ventral fin, for lateral stability to overcome the wind drift
on the floats—a tail like a miniature version of the Lockheed Constellation.

Howard DGA15, Nightingale

Length: 24'10" (7.57 m)   *Wingspan:* 38' (11.58 m)   *Cruising
speed:* 180 mph (290 km/h)

Very rare. Everything about this plane is heavy, oversized: *Large
radial in smooth cowling; big propeller spinner; heavy gear, always
with wheel pants; fixed two-rung ladder; tall tail fin;* nearby, the
V-struts enter a distinct underwing fairing.

Developed from a long-distance racer design, the D(amn) G(ood)
A(irplane) 15 was produced from 1939 (50 civilian versions) to
1942 (500 military models). Exceptionally roomy, it was a flying
ambulance for the Navy (Nightingale) and a multipurpose trainer.
High-powered, not easy to fly, not particularly forgiving. It's print-
able nickname was "Ensign Eliminator."

Curtiss–Wright Robin

Length: 24' (7.31 m)   *Wingspan:* 41' (12.5 m)   *Cruising speed:*
85 mph (137 km/h)

One of the rarest high-wing planes illustrated. *Enormous wing,
not only long, but with a 6-foot constant chord. Curious wing
braces are parallel with several auxiliary struts. Big wheels* on the
main gear; *squared-off trailing edge to tail fin* is unusual in such an
antique aircraft.

Douglas "Wrong-Way" Corrigan, who had worked on Charles
Lindbergh's *Spirit of St. Louis*, made the Curtiss–Wright Robin
forever immortal (accounting for the large interest in restoring and
recreating the 1928–1930 aircraft) by "accidentally" flying one
from Long Island, New York, to Ireland in 1938—he always maintained that he was trying to fly nonstop to Los Angeles, but his
compass reversed and he flew 180 degrees off course. Built to seat
three: the pilot followed by a pair of wicker seats that could be
offset to keep shoulders from rubbing. Corrigan flew his from a
rear seat, peering over an auxiliary gas tank in the front seat.

HIGH-WING SINGLES

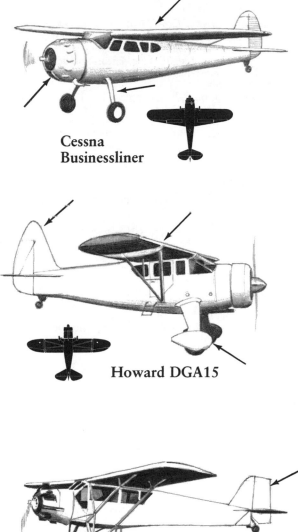

Cessna
Businessliner

Howard DGA15

Curtiss–Wright
Robin

Stinson Reliant, AT-19 (V77)

Length: 27'10" (8.48 m)   *Wingspan:* 41'11" (12.77 m)   *Cruising speed:* 120 mph (193 km/h)

Uncommon. A *masssive braced high-wing, always with cowled radial engine.* Typical wing has a single strut; earliest models a pair of almost parallel struts. *Unique wing shape: swollen over strut area,* gives the illusion of a *gull-wing.* Earliest models also have a "corrugated" cowling; typical surplus AT-19s and all late models have a smooth cowling.

The gull-wing Stinson Reliants appeared in 1935, continuing until 1942 as the lend-lease trainer and transport designated AT-19, used for radio and radar training in Great Britain. One of the earliest four- to five-seaters, it was not an uncommon short-haul airliner and company executive plane. A few battered models still flying as bush planes.

Monocoupe 90

Length: 20'6" (6.25 m)   *Wingspan:* 32' (9.75 m)   *Cruising speed:* 115 mph (185 km/h)

Quite rare. Something about this *V-braced, high-winged, radial-engined* aircraft catches the eye. It is extremely short, but *wide-cabined, with very narrow rear fuselage; cowling bumps over cylinder heads; very small propeller spinner.*

Designed in Moline, Illinois, in the golden age of amateur enthusiasm. Built from 1930 to 1942. Extremely agile little plane, used successfully in aerobatic and closed-course racing during the 1930s. Once the most popular high-performance small plane, it sat two in side-by-side comfort. Charles A. Lindbergh, who could fly anything he wanted, owned a Monocoupe.

Fairchild 24, UC-61 Forwarder (Argus)

Length: 23'9" (7.23 m)   *Wingspan:* 36'4" (11.07 m)   *Cruising speed:* 120 mph (193 km/h)

No longer common. *Roomy, high-backed fuselage* gives the impression of a small airliner; *V-braced high wing has a return strut to the wing root; notch* (for visibility) *in wing over windshield is unique,* so is the landing gear brace: *one wheel brace from fuselage, other from wing brace.*

Built from 1932 to 1947, including several hundred wartime UC-61s. About half the production was with a large radial engine, but most of those still flying are the illustrated in-line types. However, the field marks are consistent. Unusually roomy interiors sat four in military and post–1938 models. The sleek design was influenced by Raymond Loewy, creator of the Coke bottle and the Super Chief train.

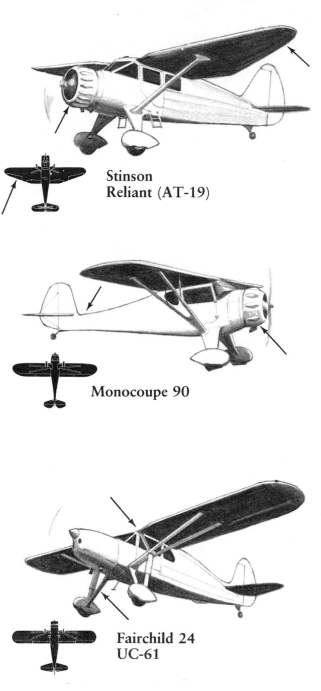

**Stinson
Reliant (AT-19)**

Monocoupe 90

**Fairchild 24
UC-61**

Rearwin Skyranger

Length: 21'9" (6.6 m)   *Wingspan:* 34' (10.36 m)   *Cruising speed:*
100 mph (161 km/h)

Very rare. This *small, fabric-covered, high-winged tail-dragger* is
best singled out by a *disproportionately large tail fin and single
side window.*

Never manufactured in large numbers (some 350 between 1940
and 1946), the little Skyranger was a comfortably furnished sport
plane that came on the market at the time that most manufacturers
were dedicating their efforts to the pre–WWII pilot training pro-
grams. Sat two, side by side, with standard dual controls, and, for
the time, an unusual "slotted" wing that gave aileron control at exceptionally low speeds. It has a landing speed of 48 mph.

Fleet Canuck

Length: 22'5" (6.83 m)   *Wingspan:* 34' (10.36 m)   *Cruising
speed:* 85 mph (137 km/h)

Rare, except in Canada. Not just another *V-braced constant-
chord* (width) *high-wing.* A much jauntier look than the similarly
sized Piper Cub; more like the very similar Taylorcraft Model B
(page 64). Close by, note the *rectangular side window with trailing
triangular quarter window.* Compare windows and tail fin shape
with Taylorcraft before deciding.

Just over 200 built from 1946 to 1951. A popular light bush
plane and a common club and trainer for Canadians—the least expensive plane available and built in Canada to boot. Somewhat over-
built for strength, it was not certified for aerobatics, but more than
one owner has looped it. Hard to stall or spin, with a leisurely
landing speed of 44 mph.

Stinson Sentinel, L-5

Length: 24'1" (7.34 m)   *Wingspan:* 34' (10.37 m)   *Cruising
speed:* 115 mph (185 km/h)

Rare. One of the few aircraft whose total impression is more distinct than individual field marks. The relatively *massive, sweeping
tail,* much like a B-17 tail fin; the *upturned nose;* and the *sweeping
belly curve from nose to tail* are distinctive. Close by, note the
unique cross-bracing of the side windows, making *three triangular
panes.* A very few of these have been converted by civilian owners
to normal-looking cockpit canopies.

From 1941 to 1944, 5000 were built. The "Flying Jeep" was the
second most common "grasshopper" in the U.S. armed forces,
right behind the Piper L-4. Sat two in tandem, but with a hinged
rear canopy it served as a flying stretcher-bearer. General George
Patton, among others, had an L-5 as a personal aircraft.

HIGH-WING SINGLES

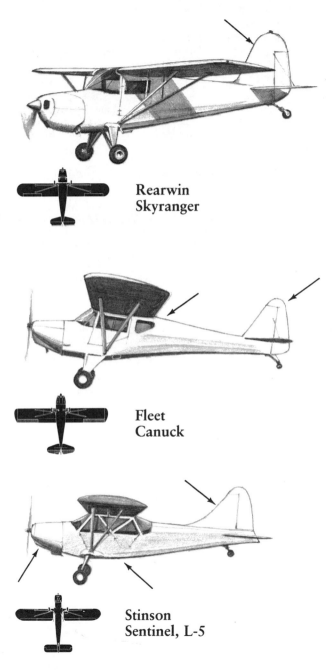

Rearwin
Skyranger

Fleet
Canuck

Stinson
Sentinel, L-5

Cessna L-19 or O-1 Bird Dog, Ector Mountaineer

Length: 25'10" (7.89 m) *Wingspan:* 36' (10.9 m) *Cruising speed:* 105 mph (169 km/h)

Not common. *An uncomplicated little single-brace, high-wing tail-dragger; almost vertical windshield; wraparound rear window; curiously noncongruent side windows; noticeable* (2.8-degree) *wing dihedral.*

More than 3000 Bird Dogs were built from 1950 to 1958, many in civilian use. The Ector Mountaineer is a 1980s revival, built from off-the-shelf or reconditioned parts and more powerful engines. Ector also builds the float brackets in as a standard item. Whether Bird Dog or Ector, the odd windows and the all-metal skin make it fairly easy to identify.

Maule Rocket, Strato-Rocket, Lunar Rocket

Length: 22' (6.71 m) *Wingspan:* 29'8" (9.04 m) *Cruising speed:* Lunar Rocket, 156 mph (251 km/h)

Not common. *A chunky four-seater, V-braced, high-wing tail-dragger.* V-bracing is simple, without return or supplementary braces. *Funny little close-out* (drag-reducing) *fairings behind wheels,* like Mercury's winged heels. Whether new (top drawing) or old (partial sketch), an *unusually large tail fin* for such a short aircraft. All models with distinctly *drooping wing tips.* Engine nacelles vary with the variety of engines supplied. Wings are short and wide compared to other constant-chord types.

In production since 1963. More recent models have powerful engines and outstanding short-field landing ability—400-foot (122 m) takeoff and landing rolls. The variance between maximum speed, 170 mph (273 km/h), and landing speed with flaps, 40 mph (65 km/h), is as great as you will find in a civilian aircraft.

Champion/Bellanca Citabria, Scout, Decathlon

Length: 22'8" (6.91 m) *Wingspan:* 33'5" (10.19 m) *Cruising speed:* 125 mph (201 km/h)

Of the small, *V-braced, constant-chord, square-end winged* planes on this page, the Citabria is best distinguished by its *fancy wheel pants* and *squared-off tail fin.*

Champion Aircraft was manufacturing the tail-dragging Champion Traveller before it shifted to this version in 1964, with its more modern tail surfaces and wheel treatment, plus strengthening that made it certifiable as an aerobatic plane (Citabria is Airbatic, backward). One of the first planes capable of continued inverted flight. From 1970 to 1980, Bellanca also built a nonaerobatic Scout and a strengthened, fully aerobatic Decathlon.

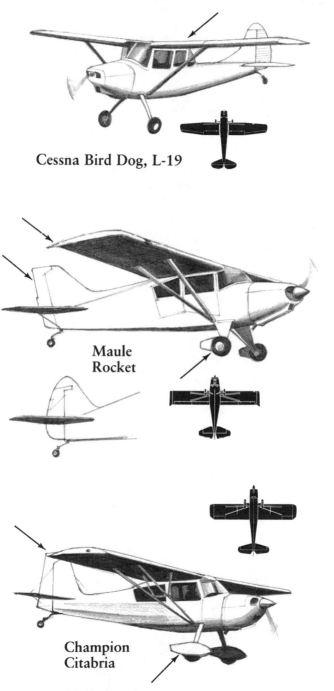

HIGH-WING SINGLES

Cessna Bird Dog, L-19

Maule
Rocket

Champion
Citabria

Arctic Tern, Interstate Cadet (L-6)

Length: 24' (7.32 m)   *Wingspan:* 36' (10.97 m)   *Cruising speed:* 115 mph (185 km/h)

Not common. Another of those darned *constant-chord, V-braced, high-wing tail-draggers.* A tandem-seat, slim plane whose most distinguishing feature is the *tall, pointy tail fin, with noticeable trim-tab showing at tail plane level.* New versions (top drawing) have squared-off wing tips; older Interstates and L-6s have round tips. The 2 *degrees of dihedral in the wing* are, as usual, quite noticeable.

Very few of the originals survive, including the L-6 (not illustrated), which was an Interstate Cadet (bottom sketch) with a greenhouse-type cockpit window. Interstate Cadets produced from 1937 to 1942 as trainers; L-6 until 1944. The design was revived in 1969 in Alaska, where the Arctic Tern (top drawing) continues to be bench-built, but with three visible changes: square wing tips, angular rear passenger window, and tail wheel moved all the way to the rear.

Funk (Akron) Model B to Model L

Length: 20' (6.1 m)   *Wingspan:* 35' (10.7 m)   *Cruising speed:* 100 mph (161 km/h)

Quite rare. One of the two *braced high-wing singles with a pair of parallel braces* (see the Porterfield Collegiate, page 62). Head on, the Funk engine cowling is quite unique, showing *round air intake completely surrounding propeller spinner. Massive tail fin; squat, chunky overall appearance.*

Built from 1939 to WWII and again from 1946 to 1948. A side-by-side two-seater that was considered remarkably easy to fly, responsive, but stable (note the large high-lift wing and the substantial stabilizing tail assembly).

Stinson 10A (Voyager 90), Voyager 108, Voyager 108-1,2,3

Length: 22' (6.71 m)   *Wingspan:* 34' (10.37 m)   *Cruising speed:* 108 mph (174 km/h).

Not common, and not just another braced high-wing tail-dragger. Though the Voyager's general shape is unique, concentrate on some fairly trivial field marks for positive identification. All the Voyagers have a noticeable (2-degree) dihedral in the wing.

Voyager 90, model 10A (top drawing): The two-seat side-by-side, with a possible third bench seat behind the pilot. *The V-brace to the wing* is quite unusual in that it has *no supplementary cross or up-braces* (contrast a typical Piper Cub). *Tail plane is set extremely low.* Although distinctly a fabric-covered plane, the general effect is clean and neat, if stubby. Built from 1939 to 1942, when it was replaced by the military L-5 (page 56).

Voyager 108 (bottom drawing): The four-seat Voyager, built from 1946 to 1948, looks much sleeker and slimmer than the Voyager 90 and has a *longer engine cowling,* housing an engine twice as powerful as the pre-war Voyager's. Same *simple V-brace* without any supplements.

Voyager 108-3 (bottom sketch): The last Voyager, with the *much larger, vertical-style tail.* Seats four. A few of the 108-3s were built by Piper until 1950.

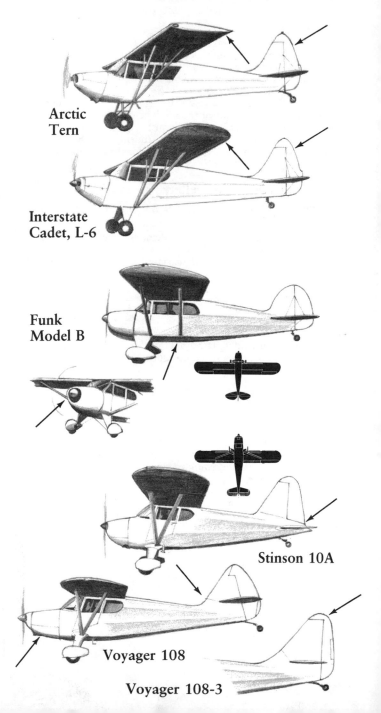

HIGH-WING SINGLES

Arctic
Tern

Interstate
Cadet, L-6

Funk
Model B

Stinson 10A

Voyager 108

Voyager 108-3

Porterfield Collegiate

Length: 22'8" (6.9 m)   *Wingspan:* 34'9" (11 m)   *Cruising speed:* 100 mph (161 km/h).

Quite rare. One of two *high-wing singles with parallel double struts.* Compare with Funk (Akron) Model B (above), a much chunkier, squatter aircraft with a larger tail fin. All fabric. If there was nothing left of a Collegiate but the engine cowling, you could identify it by the *distinct cut-in for engine exhaust.*

A tandem-seat trainer and sportster; only about 500 built before WWII put Porterfield out of the airplane business and into manufacturing troop gliders in preparation for the invasion of Europe. As a trainer, extremely popular with students; with hands off, it would recover from spins or stalls and, for the nervous, could land at speeds as low as 40 mph (64 km/h).

Aeronca Champ, Traveller, Tri-Traveller, L-16

Length: 21'6" (6.56 m)   *Wingspan:* 35' (10.66 m)   *Cruising speed:* 90 mph (145 km/h)

Very similar to the Aeronca Tandem, and the Aeronca Chief; separate from the Tandem by the Champ's *smooth engine cowling,* from the Chief by the slimmer fuselage/cabin, indicating its tandem seating.

Built from 1948 to 1964, the last dozen years by the Champion Aircraft Company, which acquired the design from Aeronca. Military observation versions (L-16) had four large, square side windows, otherwise identical. Champion Aircraft called it the Traveller and also manufactured more than 1000 Tri-Travellers, a popular flight instruction model. The Tri-Traveller sits on its tricycle gear with its nose distinctly turned up, quite noticeable on the flight line.

Aeronca Chief, Super Chief

Length: 21' (6.3 m)   *Wingspan:* 36' (10.9 m)   *Cruising speed:* 95 mph (153 km/h)

A pair of somewhat *stubby, braced high-wing two-seaters.* Like so many WWII planes, it's of *fabric construction,* with constant-chord (width) wings and rounded tips. Close at hand, *Aeronca's trailing edge of the tail fin shows a noticeable extrusion*—an adjustable trim-tab. Once you've positively noted this, you'll find the shape of the entire plane sufficiently distinctive for long-range identification. The *Super Chief tail is much larger* (bottom sketch). The *Champion is very similar; its slimmer fuselage indicates the tandem-seating for two.*

The original Chief was designed to take Continental's revolutionary opposed four-cylinder engine; first flown in 1938. With side-by-side seating for two, it was cosier than contemporary tandems, including the popular Piper Cubs. The Chief production ended in 1948. The Super Chief was built between 1946 and 1950.

Porterfield
Collegiate

Aeronca
Champ

Aeronca
Chief

Super
Chief

Aeronca 15AC Sedan

Length: 25'3" (7.70 m)   *Wingspan:* 37'6" (11.43 m)   *Cruising speed:* 114 mph (183 km/h)

A rare *high-wing tail-dragger:* The *single-wing brace attaches much farther outboard* than somewhat similar Cessna high-wings. The distinctive *tail fin appears to lean forward and shows the typical Aeronca bump.*

Never common, the Sedan (close at hand, note the automobile-style door and window configuration) was built from 1947 to 1950. Perhaps 120 are still flying, some on floats. A roomy four-seater with good "high and hot" flying characteristics, it's capable of taking off with less than 500 feet of ground roll at sea level. Came standard with dual controls.

Taylorcraft Model B, Taylorcraft F19 and F21 Sportsman

Length: 22'1" (6.73 m)   *Wingspan:* 36' (10.97 m)   *Cruising speed:* 115 mph (185 km/h).

A variety of airplanes, based on a pre–WWII design, but in production as late as 1982. *Large, upright tail fin with a distinct flat spot on the rudder; long, slim fuselage appears to "pinch down" to the tail assembly.* Compare carefully with Taylorcraft Model D and L-2 Grasshopper (next drawing). Lowest-priced Model Bs lacked the rear quarter-window.

The classic Model B Taylorcrafts, built from 1938 to 1958, lacked such niceties as wheel pants; so did the Taylorcraft F19 Sportsman, built by the revived company in 1968 (top drawing). Most sat two side by side, but a few were built in the 1950s to seat four. The revived Taylorcraft F19, and the last model, the wheel-panted (or, as they say in Britain, the "spatted-wheel") F21, returned to the two-seater format.

Taylorcraft Model D, L-2, O-57

Length: 22'1" (6.73 m)   *Wingspan:* 36' (10.97 m)   *Cruising speed:* 90 mph (145 km/h)

Fairly common. Compare closely to the Taylorcraft Model B, noting that it has the same large tail with a flat spot on the rudder. Always with *exposed cylinder heads* (but so were a few Model Bs). If tandem seating is visible, that separates it from the Model Bs; so does the A-shaped supplementary brace from the V-brace to the wing (Model B and F19 and F21 have a rectangular supplementary brace).

The L-2, with *greenhouse canopy and cut-down fuselage* (bottom sketch), was a popular war-surplus purchase.

There was no advantage to retooling from the dual control Model B trainers to the Model D Tandem trainer, except that it was the general wisdom that instructors should ride behind, not next to, the student. Several thousand Tandems and L-2s (also known as O-57) were built from 1941 to 1945.

HIGH-WING SINGLES

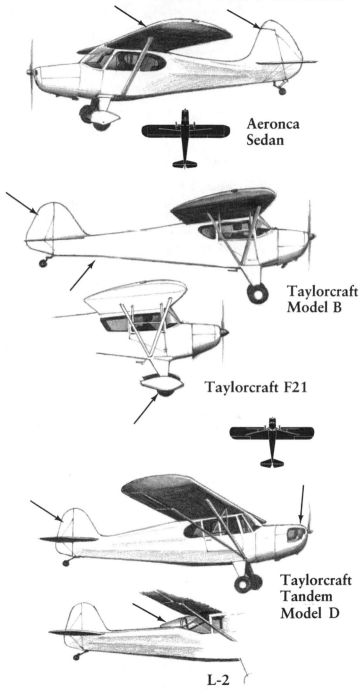

Aeronca
Sedan

Taylorcraft
Model B

Taylorcraft F21

Taylorcraft
Tandem
Model D

L-2

Aeronca Tandem 65T, L-3

Length: 22'4" (6.8 m)   *Wingspan:* 35' (10.6 m)   *Cruising speed:* 80 mph (130 km/h)

Not common. Shares some field marks with early Piper Cubs. *Engine cylinders show through cowling* (as on Piper J3) but Tandem's cowling looks pug-nosed. A small *triangular brace was added to main wing braces. Tail rounded* (note flat spot on Piper J3 Cub tail). The rear window shape is unique.

The Tandem was designed in 1940 for the pre–WWII Civilian Pilot Training Program—it's basically an Aeronca Chief with tandem seating. The rear seat, in a useful invention, was suspended six inches higher than the front seat, for visibility. The Army Air Force ordered thousands of Tandems with extra windows (bottom sketch) as the L-3, a liaison and observation airplane.

Piper J3 Cub Trainer, PA11 Cub Special, J5 Cub Cruiser, PA12 Super Cruiser, J4 Cub Coupe

Length: 22'4" (6.80 m)   *Wingspan:* 35'3" (10.74 m)   *Cruising speeds:* J3, 80 mph; Super Cruiser, 100 mph (129–161 km/h)

Not every *constant-chord* (width) *high-wing, fabric tail-dragger* is a Cub; it just seems that way.

J3 (top drawing): *Exposed cylinder heads* (compare Aeronca Tandem, L-3), *V-brace, and distinct flat spot on tail.* Some 5000 built before WWII. A popular tandem-seat, two-man trainer that introduced nearly 75 percent of WWII aviators to flying, mostly through the Civilian Pilot Training Program. More than 5000 built for WWII observation-liaison as L-4.

PA11 Cub Special, J5 Cub Cruiser, PA12 Super Cruiser (middle sketch): In spite of a variety of engines and names, these are all *three-seaters* (one pilot seat, and two passenger seats to the rear), with *fully enclosed engine.* Several hundred still flying, particularly the higher-powered Super Cruisers; many on floats. About 6000 built of the various three-seaters.

J4 Cub Coupe (bottom drawing): Rarest of all. Compare closely to Super Cub (next entry) before deciding. *Engine cowling shows a distinct bump over cylinder heads* (compare middle sketch and Super Cub drawing), *a pudgy, dumpy look* caused by stuffing a side-by-side two-person cockpit onto the slim J3 Cub fuselage, which was designed for tandem seating. The J4 Cub Coupe tail is more rounded than the J3, etc., making it quite similar to Super Cub tail.

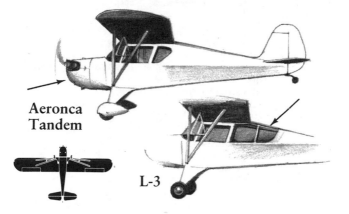

Aeronca
Tandem

L-3

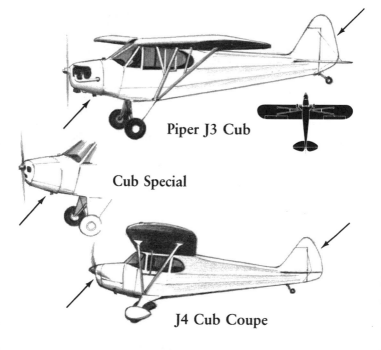

Piper J3 Cub

Cub Special

J4 Cub Coupe

Piper PA18 Super Cub, L-18

Length: 22'7" (6.88 m)   *Wingspan:* 35'2" (10.73 m)   *Cruising speed:* 115 mph (185 km/h)

Common as crabgrass. *Tail-dragging, all-fabric, rounded-tip, constant-chord* (width), *braced high-wing,* with *smooth cowling completely enclosing engine.* Compare the J3 and Cub Cruiser (previous entry). *Always something showing below propeller spinner—* a location Piper has used for a variety of engine air intakes, landing lights, etc., all absent on the earlier Cubs.

First flown in 1949, kept in production (from inventory parts) as late as 1982, although dropped from Piper's official list that year. The success of the tandem two-seat Super Cub with standard dual controls was unquestioned—more than 30,000 were sold in the first 22 years of production. While the Super Cub endured, the various three- and four-seat Cubs were dropped in favor of new low-wing designs. The Super Cub, with more sophisticated construction methods (metal instead of wood wing spars, for example), is still essentially a power upgrade of the old tandem, two-seat J3. Now built by WTA, Inc., Lubbock, Texas.

Luscombe 8A-8F, Silvaire

Length: 20' (6.09 m)   *Wingspan:* 35' (10.66 m)   *Cruising speed:* 105 mph (169 km/h)

Uncommon. A *small all-metal* plane, usually finished in *plain polished aluminum.* Strong men refer to it as "dainty" and "beautiful." Pre-war models had fabric-covered wings. Wings show slight tapers toward the tip, separating it quickly from its constant-chord cohort. A distinct notch in the trailing edge of the wing over the cockpit is visible; it's similar to biplane upper wings. Compare the Cessna 140 before being sure.

A pure sport and touring two-seater, designed in 1937 by Don Luscombe, author of the Monocoupe light plane design. Only 1200 built before WWII, but more than 5000 built from 1945 to 1949 by Luscombe. A few more built by Temco, and some bench-built by Silvaire as recently as 1960. Drawing shows the original 8A to 8D models with V-strut; 8E onward had a single strut.

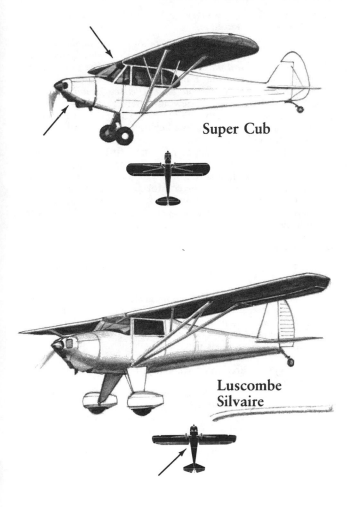

Super Cub

Luscombe
Silvaire

Cessna 120, 140

Length: 21'6" (6.58 m)   *Wingspan:* 32'10" (10 m)   *Cruising speed:* 105 mph (169 km/h)

Still common. *A braced high-wing, tail-dragging single. Most with two braces on a constant-chord* (width) *wing with rounded tip. Deeply recurved tail planes, rounded tail fin.* The model 120 was a stripped-down version, but the only visible difference is that the *120 lacks the quarter-window behind passenger window.* In 1949–1950, the 140D had the new all-metal Cessna wing and a single brace—it looks exactly like the model 170 (lower drawing), but with a smaller quarter-window behind the door, and no dorsal fin fairing to the tail fin.

Introduced in 1946, the two-seat Cessna 120/140 was one of the least expensive and highest-powered (85 hp) private airplanes you could buy. The spraddling spring-steel landing gear was so bouncy that the plane was actually more comfortable on grass strips than paved runways, and it matched up nicely with the pasture pilots and small grass airports that were typical of the late 1940s. Nearly 5000 built by 1950, when production ended.

Cessna 170

Length: 25' (7.62 m)   *Wingspan:* 36' (10.96 m)   *Cruising speed:* 110 mph (177 km/h)

Still common. *An all-metal, tail-dragging, braced high-wing single with spring-steel landing gear. The rounded tail fin merging into a long dorsal fin is unique* (other planes with the dorsal fin leading into the tail have more angular tail fins). A few (less than 10 percent) are early models with constant-chord wing and two wing struts, and without the dorsal fin: They resemble the 120/140 (previous entry) but are larger overall, with a much larger rear quarter-window.

The 170 was essentially a trade-up to four seats from the extremely popular Cessna 140. After one year (1948) the company introduced the all-metal tapered wing and subsequently sold nearly 5000 170s. It became the Cessna 172 after eight years of production by the simple addition of a tricycle gear and an angular, less romantic tail fin. Some 170s, meant for paved-only use, have wheel pants on the main gear.

Cessna 208 Caravan

Length: 37'7" (11.46 m)   *Wingspan:* 51'8" (15.75 m)   *Cruising speed:* 214 mph (344 km/h)

New in 1984. *A monster single,* comparable to the de Havilland Otter in size; *single Cessna-style brace to wing; five passenger windows; angular tail surfaces.*

The Caravan, with a single turbocharged 600-horsepower engine, carrying up to 14 people, is an attempt to find a replacement for the no-longer-manufactured de Havilland Otters and Beavers and the many Cessna 180s and 185s. The tall fixed gear is meant for unimproved airstrips. Sales to military services are expected, as ambulance, parachute, and light transport. It can carry a ton and a half of freight more than 1000 miles.

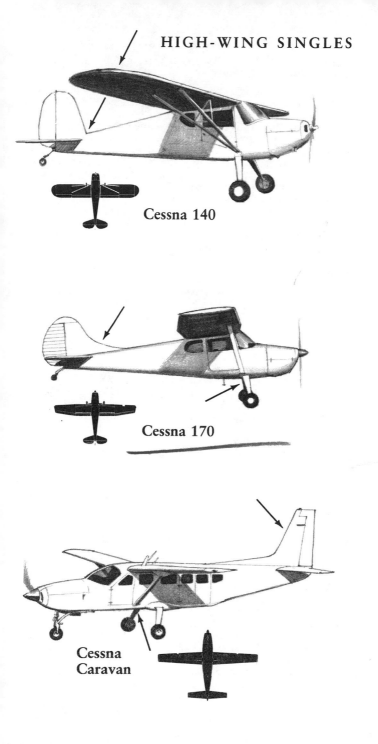

HIGH-WING SINGLES

Cessna 140

Cessna 170

Cessna
Caravan

Cessna 180/185 Skywagon, Carryall, Agwagon

Length: 25'9" (7.85 m)   *Wingspan:* 35'10" (10.92 m)   *Cruising speed:* 129 mph (208 km/h)

A *large tail-dragger,* with *braced high wing.* Size, and the presence of three side windows, separates it from the 140/170 (page 70). Has a substantial tail—slightly smaller on the model 180 than on the 185—but this is difficult to determine the first time, unless the planes are side by side. After you've seen them both, it's quite noticeable.

In constant production, with minor changes (windows, engines, and making the drooping wing tip standard on recent models) since 1953. The big-tailed, six-seat 185, first produced in 1961, is a very common float plane in the north woods. There are standard spray-boom-equipped models for agricultural use; these show not only the booms, but a 160-gallon spray tank that attaches to the fuselage under the cockpit. The slight (less than 2-degree) dihedral in the wing is quite noticeable.

Helio Courier, U-10

Length: 31' (9.45 m)   *Wingspan:* 39' (11.89 m)   *Cruising speed:* 150 mph (241 km/h)

Not common. *Unbraced high, constant-chord* (width) *wing;* usually a tail-dragger; a very few with fixed tricycle gear. On tail-draggers, the *forward gear is on extremely long struts and is set well forward of the wing. Very tall, upright tail fin.*

Manufactured from 1955 to 1978, about half the small production went to the U.S. Air Force as U-10s, a common liaison, cargo, and anti-insurgency plane in the Vietnam War. The only airplane completely designed by Harvard and Massachusetts Institute of Technology faculty members. Full-length leading-edge slotted flaps and massive slotted trailing-edge flaps give it a bizarre short takeoff and landing capability. Seats up to six. Whatever the gear or engine type, the tail and wing configurations are consistent.

Piper PA20 Pacer, PA22 Tri-Pacer, PA15 Vagabond

Length: 20'4" (6.2 m)   *Wingspan:* 29'4" (8.9 m)   *Cruising speed:* 130 mph (209 km/h)

A set of *braced high-wing singles* with *two struts to wing* (compare similar Cessnas, with a single brace). *Wings similar in shape, but much stubbier than on the Piper Cub and Super Cub.* The Tri-Pacer (top drawing) also shows a large air scoop over the nose gear.

Piper, which had been building the very successful tandem-seat Cub series, decided to add another low-cost item in 1948 and 1949, the fabric-winged PA15 Vagabonds, side-by-side two-seaters. These quickly grew into the four-seat Pacers, with more powerful engines than the Cubs. The much stubbier Pacer wing (about three-quarters the total area of the Cub wing) did allow the Pacer to fly about 20 mph faster than the comparable Cub. Because of the lack of lift in the shorter wing, it climbed about two-thirds as fast as the Cub.

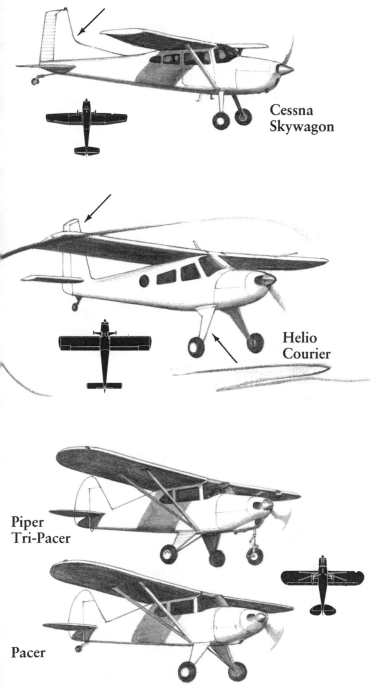

Cessna
Skywagon

Helio
Courier

Piper
Tri-Pacer

Pacer

Cessna 150, 152

Length: 24'1" (7.34 m)   *Wingspan:* 33'2" (10.11 m)   *Cruising speed:* 120 mph (193 km/h)

A series of *small braced high-wing* planes; all two-seaters; commonly fitted with dual controls for training. From 1970 onward, an optional version (the Aerobat) had structural strengthening for aerobatic flying—these will have a pair of cockpit ceiling through-the-wing windows. Some 30,000 150s and 152s were built (most of them resembling the top drawing). Many converted to tail-draggers.

Model 150A, B, C (bottom drawing): Note *two side windows* and *upright tail fin.* About 3000 built from 1959 to 1963.

Model 150D (not illustrated): Built only in 1964; has the single side window and wraparound rear window of the late Model 150s and all Model 152s (top drawing) but with the upright tail fin of the earlier 150s.

Model 150s built from 1965 to 1977, and all Model 152s built from 1978 to date (top drawing): *Single side window, wraparound rear window, swept tail fin.* The 1965 150Es had a shorter dorsal fin fairing into the swept tail.

North American Rockwell Darter Commander, Lark Commander

Length: Lark, 27'2" (8.28 m)   *Wingspan:* 35' (10.67 m)   *Cruising speed:* 130 mph (209 km/h)

Rare. *Constant-chord wings, with square tips; tricycle gear.* Darter Commander (upper sketch) is 5 feet shorter and has *upright angular tail fin.* Lark Commander (main drawing) stretched the fuselage and added *swept tail fin.*

Odd little four-seaters: designed by the Volaire company, which was acquired by Aero Commander, which was acquired by Rockwell. From 1968 to 1971, Rockwell built fewer than 200, as the parent company switched to low-wing designs in single-engine aircraft (the Aero Commander 112). Intended to compete with the Cessna 150, of which more than 10,000 had been delivered before the Darter/Lark came on the market.

HIGH-WING SINGLES

Cessna 152

Cessna 150

Aero Darter
Commander

Aero Commander
Lark Commander

Cessna 172, 172 Skyhawk, T-41 Mescalero, 175 Skylark, Cutlass, Cutlass RG, Hawk XP

Length: 27'2" (8.28 m)   *Wingspan:* 36'1" (11 m)   *Cruising speed:* 172 Skyhawk, 140 mph (225 km/h)

Ubiquitous. A series of classic high-wing single Cessnas. Still in production, but we'll take them in order, from the 1956 introduction of the Cessna 172, essentially a 170 with tricycle landing gear:

Cessna 172 (top drawing): *Two side windows; no rear window; high, unswept tail fin, with corrugated rudder. Squared-off nose* (compare with the 182/Skylane cowling, small sketch above 172 drawing).

Cessna 172 Skyhawk (model years 1960 to 1963) and 1958 model year Skylark (lower drawing): This is the old 172 cabin configuration with *swept tail fin* and *wheel pants.*

Cessna 175 Skylark (1959 to 1962): The Skylark was distinguished, until maintenance problems killed the idea, by a geared down propeller. Note the *hump behind the propeller spinner;* otherwise identical to contemporary Skyhawks.

Cessna 172 Skyhawk (1964 to date): Drawing shows the 1982 model, with a *long dorsal fin fairing to tail fin, and wraparound rear window.* The dorsal fin was shorter when the plane was introduced; it reached this length in 1971. Distinguish it from same-age 182 Skylanes, which have a flat rear window. Skylanes are also bulkier and huskier than Skyhawks, but you should make the distinction close at hand, and then learn the conformation. Some 172s seen in blue and white paint, with "U.S. Air Force" lettered on the side, but without other insignia, in civilian-operated contract flight schools near Air Force training bases, where it is the 30-hour primary trainer, designated T-41 Mescalero.

Cessna Hawk XP (extra performance) (1978 to date): A 172 Skyhawk with fixed gear, a more powerful engine, and subtle differences in only the nose cowling. Note the *larger spinner* and the *sleek cowling, with landing lights just above the nose wheel.*

Cessna 172 Cutlass: A 180-horsepower version of the 172 Skyhawk; no visible differences.

Cessna 172 Cutlass RG: *A retractable-gear Skyhawk; wheel wells remain open.* Distinguish from the very similar, but bulkier, retractable Skylane RG by the wraparound rear windshield. After you've seen them both close at hand, the difference in their shape will be a better field mark.

HIGH-WING SINGLES

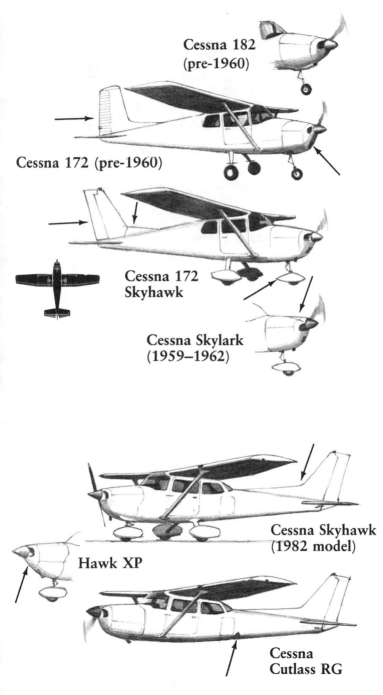

Cessna 182 (pre-1960)

Cessna 172 (pre-1960)

Cessna 172 Skyhawk

Cessna Skylark (1959–1962)

Cessna Skyhawk (1982 model)

Hawk XP

Cessna Cutlass RG

Cessna 182 Skylane, Skylane RG

Length: 28'2" (8.59 m)   *Wingspan:* 35'10" (10.92 m)   *Cruising speed:* 157 mph (253 km/h)

A *pair of identical braced high-wing singles.* One, the *RG, has retractable gear* (top drawing), which increases the cruising speed to 179 mph (289 km/h). When retracted, note the open wheel wells on each side of the fuselage. Experienced pilots often can tell the difference between the Skylanes and the Skyhawks (page 76), but not so many as think they can. Skylanes have a *flat, nonwraparound rear window.* Compare the Cessna 172 series (page 76): Early 172s lacked rear window; later types have wraparound rear window.

Various models have been in continuous production since 1956. What we have here is a more powerful version of the older model 172. But Cessna already had that in the model 180. There was an era, in the 1950s and 1960s, when manufacturers attempted to make every possible sort of light plane, with nearly insubstantial differences directed at very specific markets.

Cessna Stationair, Skywagon, and Super Skylane

Stationair 7 specifications: *Length:* 31'9" (9.68 m)   *Wingspan:* 35'10" (10.92 m)   *Cruising speed:* 156 mph (251 km/h)

Common, variable. A series of pilot plus five- or six-passenger aircraft most easily distinguished from their Cessna stablemates by sheer size; *all with single brace, wheel pants, and swept tail fins.*

Cessna 205 and 206 (Stationair 5, 6) and Super Skylane (top drawing): *three passenger windows.* The more comfortably appointed Super Skylane looks just like a Stationair 6 from the port side but has a single door, not the double cargo doors of a Stationair, on the starboard side. This group has the same wing, but a fuselage length of 28 feet (8.53 m).

Cessna 207, 208 (Stationair 7, 8) (bottom drawing): Noticeably longer, emphasized by the *four, not three, side windows.*

Until the invention of the fourteen-passenger Caravan, the Stationair 8 was the largest braced-wing Cessna, and one of the larger single-engine planes. made. It will come as no comfort to those who try to put the proper names on things to learn that the original model 206 was called a Skywagon, that the next version, the model 207, was also given that name, and that the 206 was then called a Stationair again. When the final version of the 207 came out, it was called a Stationair 8. Several thousand of all types have been built since 1964. For the real Skywagon, see page 72.

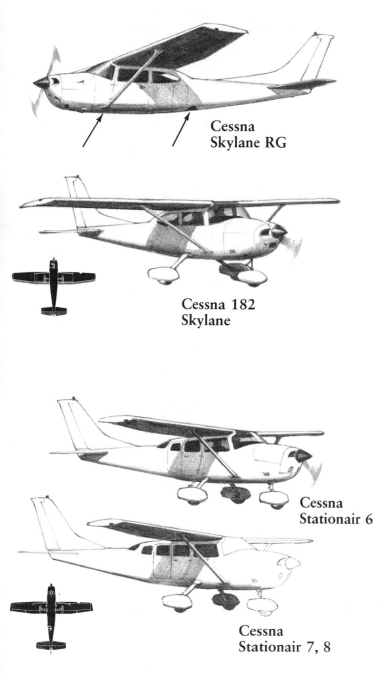

HIGH-WING SINGLES

Cessna
Skylane RG

Cessna 182
Skylane

Cessna
Stationair 6

Cessna
Stationair 7, 8

Cessna Centurion, Turbo Centurion

Length: 28'2" (8.59 m)   *Wingspan:* 36'9" (11.20 m)   *Cruising speed:* Centurion, 193 mph (311 km/h); Turbo, 222 mph (357 km/h)

An *unbraced high-wing.* The *tail plane is mounted slightly higher than on Cardinal series; two large side windows on Centurion, four small windows on pressurized Turbo Centurion* (but compare the Cardinal RG, next drawing). Almost all Centurions have a *dorsal fin that begins at the rear of the cabin* (compare shorter fin on Cardinal RG).

Seating the pilot plus six, the Centurions have been in production since 1967, and their combination of unbraced high wing and retractable gear, along with the Cardinal RG, is unique in the industry. The pressurized Centurion was added to the line in 1977. There are a few early models around, built from 1964 to 1966, which have a braced wing, that are virtually indistinguishable from a Cessna Cutlass RG (previous entry). If you see an unbraced-wing Centurion that appears to have a smaller dorsal fin than illustrated (or happen to see a pair of them parked side by side), it is one of the models built in 1967 or 1968. Centurions built from 1969 to 1978 had doors to cover the main landing gear. Models built from 1979 to date have eliminated the doors and show a distinct notch just under the rear of the cabin (typical as on lower drawing of the T210 pressurized Centurion).

Cessna Cardinal Classic, Cardinal RG

Length: 27'3" (8.31 m)   *Wing span:* 35'6" (10.82 m)   *Cruising speed:* RG, 139 mph (224 km/h)

Anything with an *unbraced wing and fixed tricycle gear is a Cardinal.* The retractable model is best distinguished from the similar Cessna Centurion by *smaller size; dorsal fin to tail begins well behind cabin* on both models; *tail plane set very low* (appears to be glued on, not inserted, as on the Centurion).

More than 4000 of these dapper little planes were built from 1967 until production ceased in 1978. (Early models were designated 177; the name "Cardinal" originally indicated a 177 with more horsepower, fancier interiors, and full blind-flying instrumentation.) The unbraced wing looks attractive, but it actually added little speed, or efficiency. Cessna found that in the four-seater business it was competing with itself, the braced-wing Cessna Skylane RG being a perfectly acceptable, slightly less expensive alternative to the Cardinal RG. The model 177 was withdrawn in 1976, followed by two years of producing only Cardinals.

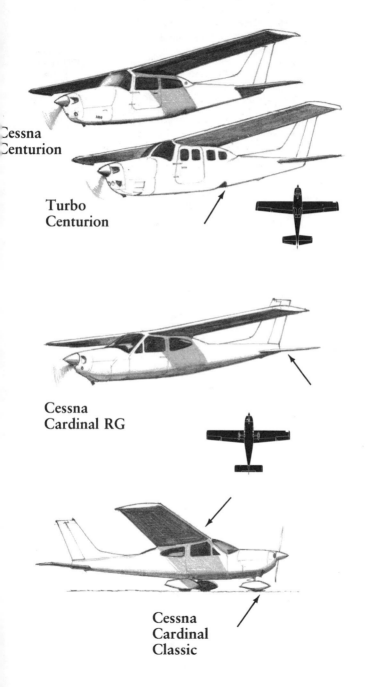

Cessna
Centurion

Turbo
Centurion

Cessna
Cardinal RG

Cessna
Cardinal
Classic

Lake LA-4 Buccaneer (and variations)

LA-4-200 specifications: *Length:* 24'11" (7.6 m)   *Wingspan:* 38' (11.6 m)   *Cruising speed:* 150 mph (241 km/h).

A series of four- to six-place amphibians.

High-winged flying boat or amphibian with a single engine mounted on pylons *high* above the cabin, with the propeller in the *pushing* position. A similar plane, with the propeller in the conventional traction position, is the TSC-1 Teal.

There are a few pure flying boat versions of this aircraft, which are the original manufacturer's Colonial Skimmer, middle sketch, first flown in 1955. The Skimmers also lack the support struts on the engine pylon. Planes produced since 1960 have been amphibian, with engines ranging from 150 to 200 horsepower. The Renegade, bottom sketch, seats five and is 28 feet 10 inches (8.79 m) long. The Buccaneer series also can be separated from the Teals by the tail plane. All Teals have a T-tail; all Skimmers and Buccaneers have a tail plane mounted midway up the tail fin.

TSC1 Teal

Teal II specifications: *Length:* 23'7" (7.19 m)   *Wingspan:* 31'11" (9.73 m)   *Cruising speed:* 115 mph (185 km/h)

Two- to four-passenger amphibian. *Traction* engine is mounted high above the fuselage on *four* struts.

In the world of flying boats, the Teals are flying canoes, especially the early Teals, although there is now a Teal III that carries up to four passengers. Any T-tailed, traction propeller, high-engined amphibian is a Teal. Teals come with standard dual controls and seats that fold up for fishermen, the aircraft's typical purchaser. First produced in 1969, the plane has been built by the designer, Thurston Aircraft, by Schweitzer, and now by the Teal Aircraft Company.

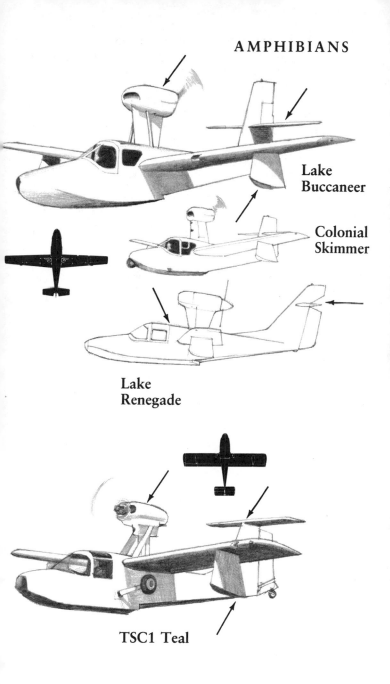

AMPHIBIANS

Lake
Buccaneer

Colonial
Skimmer

Lake
Renegade

TSC1 Teal

Republic RC3 Seabee

Length: 28' (8.53 m)   *Wingspan:* 37'8" (11.48 m)   *Cruising speed:* 105 mph (169 km/h)

A fat-cabined, thin-fuselaged amphibian with a *gently curved leading edge* to the tail fin. *Pusher propeller* mounted on the rear of the cabin. See the similar Trident Tri-Gull.

The Seagull on land is clearly a tail-dragger, and the rear wheel stays down in flight as the two front wheels retract up to, but not into, the fuselage. It was with visions of a vast postwar leisure-time market that the Republic Aviation Company purchased Percy Spencer's design for his home-built Spencer S-12 in 1943 and certified the plane in 1946. It was an era when men were seriously designing flying automobiles as well. Republic cranked out 1080 of the planes in a little more than two years, at a net loss of some $14 million. The mass market never caught up with the costs of tooling up and producing aircraft that sold for less than $6000.

Trident TR 1 Trigull 320

Length: 28'6" (8.69 m)   *Wingspan:* 41'9" (12.73 m)   *Cruising speed:* 154 mph (248 km/h)

Still rare, except in the Pacific Northwest. *Pusher engine* mounted *on, not above,* the fuselage, fat-cabined and wasp-waisted, with *straight-line tail fin.*

A modern version of the old Seabee, manufactured in British Columbia, the Trigull is clearly newer. Note the angular, rather than sculpted, lines to the fuselage and tail section. In flight, it's easily distinguished by the pontoons that fold up and become part of the wing's aerodynamic surface. The tricycle landing gear includes a nose wheel that remains visible when retracted and serves as a bumper. The plane's light weight (foam and fiber glass construction, plus the retractable pontoons) gives it a distinct performance edge over the Seabee. However, because of financing problems, many more have been ordered than delivered.

Grumman G21 Goose

Original specifications: *Length:* 38'4" (11.68 m)   *Wingspan:* 49' (14.94 m)   *Cruising speed:* 190 mph (306 km/h)

The oldest Grumman amphibian. *Fully rounded tail planes and fin* and *twin engines* that *angle out* noticeably away from the centerline of the aircraft.

The Goose is such an old design (built from 1937 to 1946) that many owners have changed such details as cockpit and fuselage windows. Many fly today with turboprops replacing the old radials and with retractable floats that fold up and become part of the wing surface in flight. But the angled-out engine position remains despite all other modifications. Crew of two and four to six passengers. Identifying the Goose is really dependent on recognizing its Grumman origins and its old-fashioned boatlike lines. The somewhat similar Grumman Widgeon is noticeably smaller, and the very rare Grumman Mallard has a distinctly upswept look to the rear fuselage. See those entries before deciding you've seen the Goose.

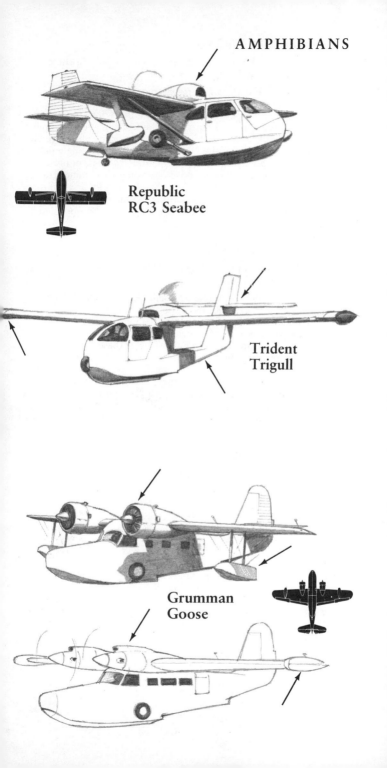

AMPHIBIANS

Republic
RC3 Seabee

Trident
Trigull

Grumman
Goose

Grumman G44 Widgeon

Length: 31'1" (9.47 m)   *Wingspan:* 40' (12.19 m)   *Cruising speed:* 130 mph (209 km/h) Mach 0.196

A small airplane with *in-line twin engines* mounted *parallel to aircraft midline;* sculpted Grumman-style fuselage.

Smallest of the twin-engine flying boats, the Widgeon saw extensive service as a patrol and antisubmarine craft in World War II. Although many have been converted to turboprops, the original Widgeon was sold with in-line engines, giving it a profile much different from the radial-engine Goose or Mallard. It is, in most respects, simply a scaled-down Goose, including the double-strut float mount; note, however, the less rounded tail fin and tail plane. Most of the 100 or so Widgeons still flying in North America have been converted by the McKinnon Company to turboprops and retractable wing-tip floats.

Grumman G73 Mallard

Length: 48'4" (14.73 m)   *Wingspan:* 66'8" (20.32 m)   *Cruising speed:* 180 mph (290 km/h)

Rare. Large, with noticeable *upswept rear fuselage* and very *high tail fin;* large *radial engines* and *solid float pylons.*

Only 59 ten-passenger Mallards were built between 1946 and 1951. Look for one of the few remaining Mallards in Louisiana's bayou country and in the Bahamas. Most of these will have conversions to turboprop engines: some have retractable floats. The only possible confusion is with the much larger (100-foot wingspan) Grumman Albatross (next entry). The Albatross fuselage is massive, compared to the Mallard, and all Albatross noses show a distinct, protruding radar dome. As a luxury flying yacht, the Mallard flew for persons as diverse as Henry Ford and King Farouk of Egypt.

Grumman G64 Albatross

Length: 61'3" (18.67 m)   *Wingspan:* 96'8" (29.46 m)   *Cruising speed:* 225 mph (362 km/h)

Scarce. *Very large,* with *twin radial engines;* sculpted, curving fuselage; *cantilever wing* (no struts).

Another "Grumman looking" aircraft, with solid pylons for the wing-tip floats and huge radial engines. The Albatross was built for air-sea rescue, patrol, and antisubmarine warfare. Note the nose radar dome, which is not seen on the smaller Grummans. The Canadair CL-215 (next entry) is almost as large as the Albatross, but, compared to a Grumman design, is all straight lines, whereas the Grummans have curves and shiplike moldings. Military versions were HU-16 in the U.S. Coast Guard, CSR-110 in the Canadian armed forces. Last military service was with U.S. Coast Guard; decommissioned in 1983.

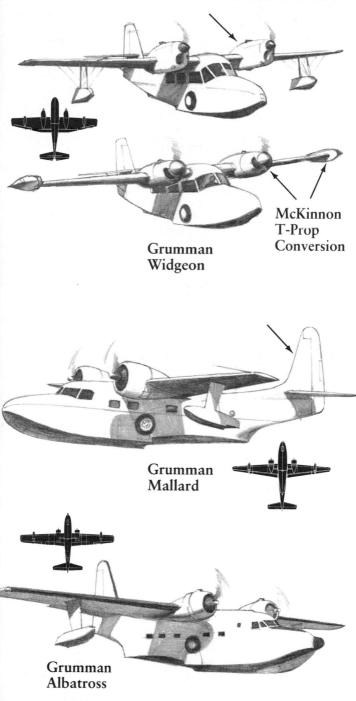

AMPHIBIANS

Grumman
Widgeon

McKinnon
T-Prop
Conversion

Grumman
Mallard

Grumman
Albatross

Canadair CL215

Length: 65' (19.81 m)   *Wingspan:* 93'10" (28.6 m)   *Cruising speed:* 181 mph (291 km/h)

Scarce. Large, with *angular tail fin* and *rectangular wing and tail planes; twin radial engines.*

The only twin-engine amphibian in production today, the CL215 was designed as a self-filling water bomber and is seen most frequently in the province of Québec, where it plays that role. There are a few passenger and cargo versions, but they are easily identified no matter what the configuration of windows and doors. All CL215s will have large radial engines (never turbos or in-lines) mounted high on the wing. None has a retractable float. The plane can land on water; pick up 1500 gallons (6 tons) of water from the lake, and take off with only 2000 feet of running room.

Convair PBY-5 and PBY-6 Catalina

Length: 63'10" (19.50 m)   *Wingspan:* 104' (31.69 m)   *Cruising speed:* 130 mph (209 km/h)

Extremely *rare.* Huge *parasol wing* braced with *wing struts; twin radial engines.* The fuselage appears to hang suspended from the wing.

Although designed in 1935, the Catalina came equipped with retractable wing floats—something available only as postproduction modifications to Grumman flying boats. Most of the original PBYs were pure flying boats; most of the survivors are amphibious. Military PBYs had blister gun ports aft of the wings and a Plexiglas gun turret in the nose (or "bow"). The few civilian modifications still around have removed the forward gun turret, though a few kept the side blisters for sightseeing flights. The PBY-6, last of the series built, is identical to the PBY-5, except for a taller, thinner tail fin. A four-engine version, the Coronado, is no longer flying.

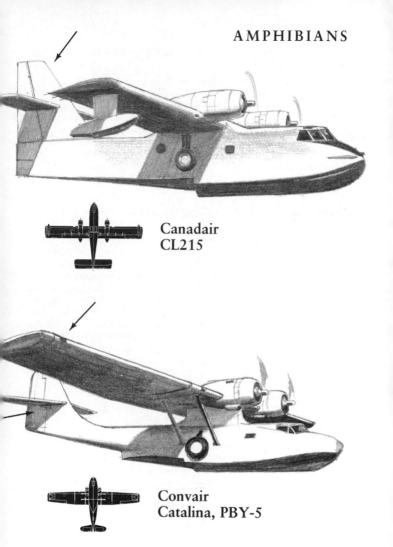

Canadair
CL215

Convair
Catalina, PBY-5

Wing D1 Derringer

Length: 23' (7.01 m)   *Wingspan:* 29'2" (8.89 m)   *Cruising speed:* 210 mph (338 km/h)

New and very rare. A *very small twin: constant-chord* (equal depth) *wing; strongly swept tail fin; molded, one-piece side and windshield; rear window in cockpit roof.*

Exhibited at the Paris Air Show in 1971, but not produced until 1980. It is of stretched metal construction, very sleek and rivetless. There is a prototype military version, intended as an inexpensive counterinsurgency plane for export to small countries. The only two-seat twin-propeller aircraft in production.

Beech Duchess 76

Length: 29'1" (8.86 m)   *Wingspan:* 38' (11.58 m)   *Cruising speed:* 175 mph (282 km/h)

Quite common. Small twin; *three side windows; one-piece curved windshield; Hershey-bar T-tail plane and wing;* more *pointy-nosed* than the comparable Piper Seminole; *distinct bullet on tail plane; engine nacelles stop at wing's trailing edge.*

Beech's entrant in the small four-seater twin market, used for multiengine training. First flown in 1974; first deliveries in 1977. The T-tail was extremely popular in the 1970s. Note the Piper Seminole and Cheyenne and the Beech Super King Air. The interest in T-tails was *perhaps* an affectation triggered by their wide use on jet airliners. Piper even added T-tails to existing single-engine models, the Lance and the Arrow. The Lance, however, reverted to a conventional tail, whereas the Arrow retained the T.

Piper PA44 Seminole

Length: 27'6" (8.39 m)   *Wingspan:* 38'7" (11.76 m)   *Cruising speed:* 192 mph (309 km/h)

A small, common twin. *T-tail; flattened engine nacelles extend slightly behind wing; two-piece windshield; three side windows of irregular geometry* (compare the small T-tail Beech Duchess 76 before deciding). The other two T-tail twins are much larger (see the Piper Cheyenne III and Beech Super King Air).

The Seminole (no relation to the U.S. Army "Seminole," their nickname for the military version of the Beech Queen Air) is a four-seat light transport and is popular as an inexpensive multi-engine trainer. Comes in a turbocharged version that is identical on the exterior, but has an altitude ceiling of 20,000 feet and a pressurized cabin.

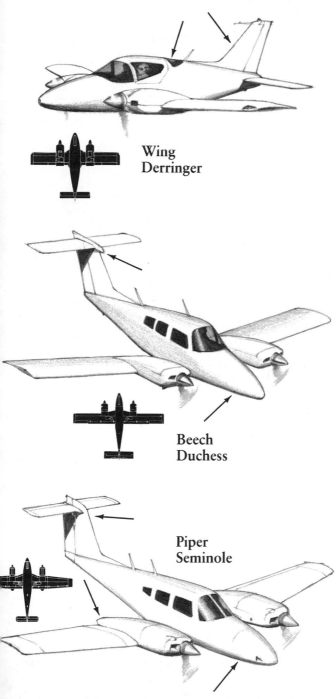

Wing
Derringer

Beech
Duchess

Piper
Seminole

Piper PA23 Apache

Length: 27'3" (8.30 m)   *Wingspan:* 37' (11.28 m)   *Cruising speed:* 150 mph (241 km/h)

Increasingly uncommon. *An old-fashioned small twin, rounded tail fin, tail planes and wing tips; two (rarely three) side windows; small engines set close to fuselage;* retracted wheels stay slightly exposed and are visible.

Built from 1954 to 1960, the first really light twin with economical engines; seats four. The wheels that do not quite retract are so built deliberately (as on many WWII bombers)—you can still land the plane if the system fails to extend the wheels; what's more, you can land, even if you forget to drop the wheels, without automatically demolishing the aircraft. Most restored models have higher horsepower engines and slightly higher cruising speeds. A few models were built with three side windows.

Piper PA23 Aztec, PA23-235 Apache

Length: 31'3" (9.52 m)   *Wingspan:* 37'3" (11.35 m)   *Cruising speed:* 204 mph (328 km/h)

A family of similar aircraft. *Conventional tail, low-wing twin; swept angular tail fin; three side windows;* noses vary in length from short (PA23-235 Apache) to medium (Aztec B, C) (top drawing) to long (Aztec D and later models). Seen overhead, the wing has complicated geometry: basically a Hershey-bar shape, but with added rounded wing tips and fairings from the fuselage to the leading edge of the wing at the engine nacelle, and from the outboard side of the engine nacelle into the wing's leading edge. The latest model, the Aztec F (bottom drawing) has an angular outline to the wing tips, as though one had simply taken the old rounded shape and snipped it two or three times with a pair of shears.

Successor to the Apache (the first Aztec in 1960 was basically an Apache with a widened cabin to seat five and a new, angular, swept tail fin), the Aztec is a six-passenger twin available with turbocharged engines. An odd characteristic, occasionally useful as a field mark when the plane is overhead and going away, is that the tail fin and tail planes trail well behind the fuselage proper.

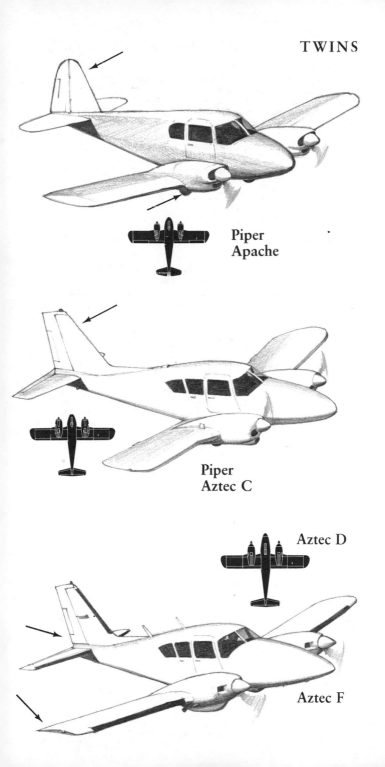

TWINS

Piper
Apache

Piper
Aztec C

Aztec D

Aztec F

Grumman American/Gulfstream American GA7, Cougar

Length: 29'10" (9.09 m)   *Wingspan:* 36'10" (11.23 m)   *Cruising speed:* 190 mph (306 km/h)

Not common; look for it at airports offering multiengine flight school. *Dihedral in wing and tail, combined with constant-chord (equal width) wing; three side windows; swept tail fin.*
First delivered in 1978, intended as an economical dual-control twin-engine trainer. Delivered as the Cougar with fancier interior. Seats four, including pilot and copilot or student. Production was sporadic, following the acquisition of Grumman American by American Jet Industries.

Piper PA34 Seneca

Length: 28'6" (8.69 m)   *Wingspan:* 38'11" (11.85 m)   *Cruising speed:* 187 mph (301 km/h)

A common sight. *Small low-wing twin; equal-chord* (width) *Hershey-bar wing and tail plane; swept tail fin.* Seneca III (illustrated) has wraparound windshield; Seneca II has a center windshield post; both have four side windows, each a different shape, diminishing to the rear. Seneca I had three larger side windows, each different in shape, and less streamlined engine nacelles. *The tail assembly seems stuck on as an afterthought:* The fin and tail planes stick out well aft of the end of the fuselage proper.
A popular five- or six-seat (including pilot) business and private aircraft. It essentially takes the single-engine Piper Cherokee SIX and substitutes two turbocharged engines. The test prototype was a Cherokee that retained the nose engine. It was flown, in fact, as a tri-motor, one of the last, and the briefest, pulling tri-motor flights in the history of aviation.

Piper PA60 Aerostar, Ted Smith Aerostar

Length: 34'10" (10.62 m)   *Wingspan:* 36'8" (11.18 m)   *Cruising speed:* 231 mph (372 km/h)

Not common, unique design. *A midwing twin; slight dihedral in wing, none in tail; leading edge of wing at right angle to fuselage, trailing edge tapers sharply to tip; tail plane strongly swept; bulbous-nosed; wraparound windshield, with two small windows above cockpit; fairing to tail fin is cut off abruptly.*
Ted Smith, a California designer, tried to build Aerostars from 1967 to 1978 in competition with the big three American builders. Although it's an attractive design and simple to construct, after several reorganizations, his company ended up as the Santa Maria Division of Piper. Typical of the Ted Smith touch, the three swept tail surfaces (fin and planes) and the three tail control surfaces are interchangeable.

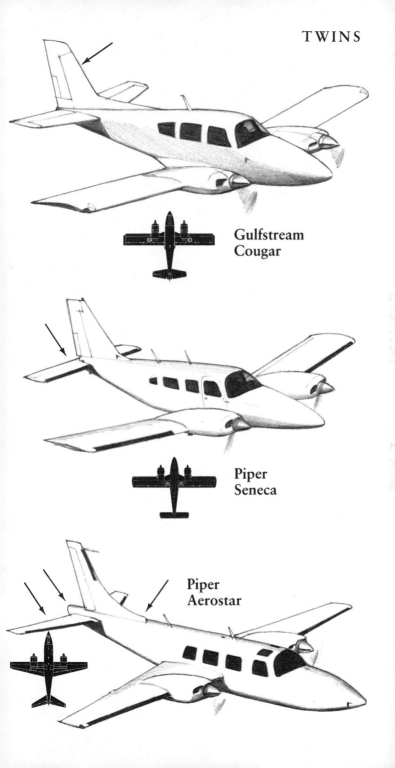

**Gulfstream
Cougar**

**Piper
Seneca**

**Piper
Aerostar**

Beech 50 Twin Bonanza, L-23 Seminole

Length: 31'6" (9.60 m)   *Wingspan:* 45'3" (13.80 m)   *Cruising speed:* 203 mph (327 km/h)

A series of *small, low-wing twins. Old-fashioned-looking vertical tail fin; dihedral in wing and tail; bulky engine nacelles house landing gear that does not retract fully.* As few as two side windows, as many as four, including the pilot's. But close at hand, note the unique *three-piece windshield,* with double divider strip in center.

Almost 1000 of these stubby little aircraft were produced from 1952 to 1961. It was the first civilian twin-engine plane available after WWII and opened up the corporate airplane market. Engine horsepower varied from 260 to 340. Could hold six passengers in seats three abreast in its chubby cockpit.

Beech 95 Travel Air

Length: 25'11" (7.90 m)   *Wingspan:* 37'10" (11.53 m)   *Cruising speed:* 195 mph (314 km/h)

Fairly common. *Very small low-wing twin; vertical tail fin; bulky nacelles; dihedral in wing, none in tail.* Landing gear retracts completely; compare Beech Twin Bonanza (previous entry). *One-piece windshield.* Close at hand, the triangular rear passenger window is unique, quite different from any Twin Bonanza.

Nearly 1000 of these little twins, the lowest priced on the market, were built from 1958 to 1968. The plane had a single-engine service ceiling of 4400 feet above sea level, which effectively eliminated it from the substantial airplane market of the Rocky Mountain and intermountain West, where airports are typically above 5000 feet.

Beech Baron 55 and Baron 58

Length: model 55, 28' (8.53 m); model 58, 29'10" (9.09 m) *Wingspan:* both, 37'10" (11.53 m)   *Cruising speed:* both, 216 mph (348 km/h)

Common. A complex series of small *low-wing piston twins.* The consistent identification marks are the typical Beech wings, with a fairing from the wing root to the engine nacelle and *dihedral in wing, none in tail.* The 55 series has three side windows, the 58, four. The *windshield is set forward of the wing's leading edge on the model 58,* sometimes a useful field mark when the wing obscures the windows. A model 58 with turboprop engines, a swept tail plane and a taller tail fin is the rare, French-built Beech Marquis, a migrant from Europe.

A small four-place (three passengers, plus pilot) aircraft of considerable popularity. More than 6000 delivered since 1960, including a few hundred of the stretched model 58 since 1970. Regular improvements were in engines, air-conditioning, and avionics rather than in airframes.

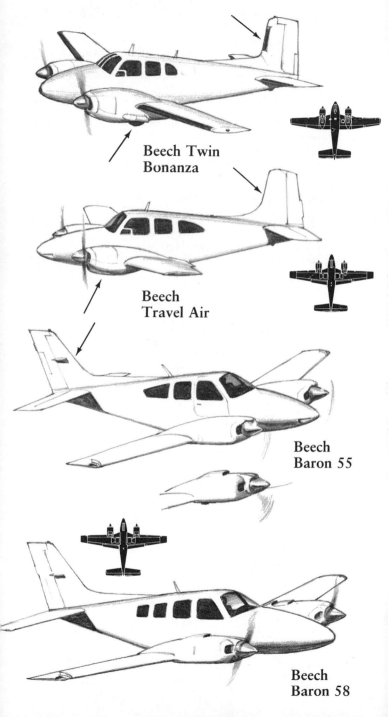

Beech Twin
Bonanza

Beech
Travel Air

Beech
Baron 55

Beech
Baron 58

Cessna T303 Crusader

Length: 30'5" (9.27 m) *Wingspan:* 39' (11.90 m) *Cruising speed:* 207 mph (333 km/h)

A *low-wing twin*, with the *tail plane mounted well up the fin; long engine nacelles trail behind wing; three rectangular passenger windows each side;* dihedral in wing, none in tail. Overhead, the wings and tail plane show symmetrical taper, with just a hint of the standard Cessna treatment: fairing from fuselage to wing's leading edge and from outboard side of engine nacelle to wing, but much less visible than on older Cessna twins.

Cessna's 1982 entry into the fuel-economic, easy-to-maintain, piston-engine business twin market. Long nose and trailing engine nacelles designed for baggage carrying. If you see it on the flight line, note that it's one of the few small twins with a stair built into the opening passenger door.

Beech B60 Duke

Length: 33'10" (10.31 m) *Wingspan:* 39'3" (11.96 m) *Cruising speed:* 250 mph (402 km/h)

A *low-wing twin piston* that shows *strong dihedral in wing and tail; long pointy nose; very strongly swept tail fin and tail plane; three rectangular windows each side.* Does not have the trailing oval passenger window typical of so many Beech aircraft; compare the Queen Air, King Air (page 108).

A four- or six-passenger plane with a crew of two, but frequently sold as a top-of-the-line personal aircraft and seldom used in the passenger business. Delivered, since 1968, as a personal and corporate aircraft. It is easily recognized at a distance by its unique lines—the illusion of speed and a certain rakishness.

Rockwell (Fuji) Commander 700

Length: 39'5" (12 m) *Wingspan:* 42'5" (12.93 m) *Cruising speed:* 252 mph (405 km/h)

A *low-winged twin; unswept and level tail plane mounted partway up fin; slim wings with dihedral;* opposed-cylinder engines carried in *flattened nacelles well forward of the wing; air scoops under nacelles for turbochargers. Trapezoidal passenger windows* (three port, four starboard) *are absolutely unique.*

A joint design of Fuji in Japan and Rockwell International in the U.S., it was first flown in 1975. Seats four to six in pressurized cabin and has a crew of two. Its practical range is more than 800 miles (1300 km). One of the few light twins built that used NACA (National Advisory Committee on Aeronautics) wing designs, though the slim and symmetrically tapering wings were constructed entirely in Japan.

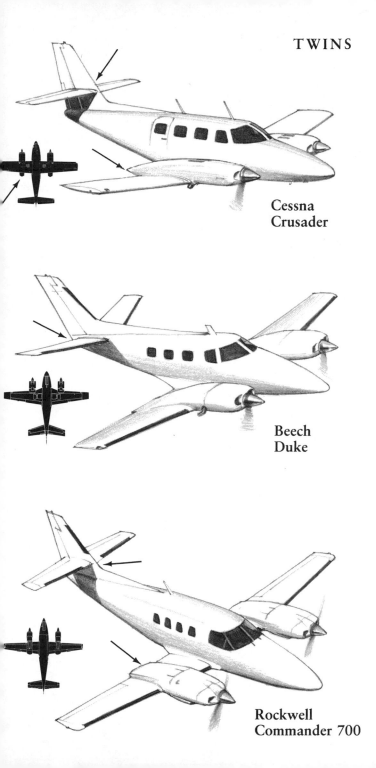

Cessna
Crusader

Beech
Duke

Rockwell
Commander 700

Piper PA31P-350 Mojave

Length: 34'6" (10.35 m)   *Wingspan:* 44'6" (13.35 m)   *Cruising speed:* 270 mph (434 km/h)

A 1983 introduction. A *low-wing twin,* with turbocharged engines in *very flattened nacelles that extend well behind the wing; dihedral in wing, none in tail; symmetrical taper both edges of wing and tail plane; three windows starboard, two port.*

A five-passenger luxury business plane with piston engines seems an odd introduction in the turboprop era, but the intent is high fuel economy and a power plant that can be worked on without a doctorate in engineering. The cabin is unusually deep for a small twin and is reflected in the bulky fuselage carried well aft. The long nose is for baggage, as are the trailing engine nacelles.

Piper PA31 Navajo, Chieftain

A family of *low-wing twins,* with *flattened engine nacelles housing opposed six-cylinder engines; no tip-tanks;* all have characteristic Piper wing: *distinct leading edge fairing from fuselage to engine nacelle, both edges taper from nacelle to wing tip; dihedral in wing, none in tail plane. Note* that the newest Chieftain commuter (PA31-350 T1040) has turboprops in round nacelles that do not extend behind the wing—essentially like Cheyenne engines. Engine nacelles on the PA31-325 Navajo and PA31-350 Chieftain extend beyond trailing edge of wing. Nacelles on PA31 Navajo and the pressurized PA31P stop well short of the trailing edge. Navajos carry six passengers; Chieftains can accommodate up to ten.

Piper PA31-325 Navajo CR (main drawing)

Length: 32'7" (9.93 m)   *Wingspan:* 40'8" (12.40 m)   *Cruising speed:* 244 mph (393 km/h)

Three large and one small side window, not counting pilot's side window; counterrotating propellers; *nacelles extend beyond trailing edge.*

Piper PA31 and PA31P (center detail sketch)

PA31 is identical to PA31-325, except *engine nacelles do not extend past trailing edge.* PA31P (pressurized) has *three windows starboard, two port* (door on port side has no window).

PA31-350 Chieftain (bottom small drawing)

Length: 34'7" (10.55 m)   *Wingspan:* 40'8" (12.40 m)   *Cruising speed:* 251 mph (404 km/h)

The stretched Navajo is common in feeder airline and air-taxi service. *Shows five windows on each side, not counting pilot's window; nacelles on most models extend beyond trailing edge,* but the less common PA31-350-T1040 has turboprops in round nacelles that do not extend past trailing edge.

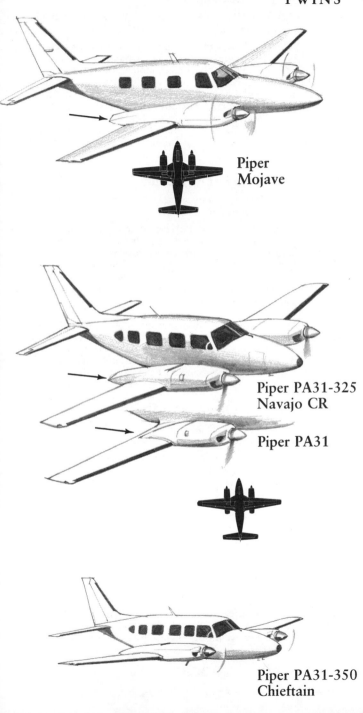

Piper
Mojave

Piper PA31-325
Navajo CR

Piper PA31

Piper PA31-350
Chieftain

Piper PA31T Cheyenne

Length: Cheyenne IIXL, 36'8" (11.18 m)   *Wingspan:* all models, 42'8" (13.01 m)   *Cruising speed:* 244 mph (393 km/h)

Fairly common. *Low-wing turboprop twin; engine nacelles blend into wing's trailing edge; swept tail fin; barely visible dihedral in wing, none in tail; tip-tanks.* The XL model illustrated has four passenger windows starboard, three port. Earlier models Cheyenne I and II are 2 feet shorter and show three- and two-passenger windows, starboard and port. A few Cheyenne I's do not have tip-tanks.

Built since 1969, the high-powered Cheyenne II is actually the typical and original Cheyenne. The Cheyenne I is a version with less powerful engines and less standard equipment that was not introduced until 1978.

Piper PA30, PA39, Twin Comanche

Length: 25'2" (7.67 m)   *Wingspan:* 36'9" (11.22 m)   *Cruising speed:* 186 mph (299 km/h)

A small *low-wing twin.* Manufactured *with and without tip-tanks; engine nacelles stop well short of trailing edge.* Though it has the characteristic Piper fairing from fuselage to engine nacelles, the leading edge is straight and the trailing edge tapered, which gives the wing the illusion of *leaning forward. Dihedral in wing, none in tail plane.* Comes with *two or* (more commonly) *three side windows, including the pilot's side window.*

A successful and popular series that first flew in 1962. All seat four persons, including the pilot. Various models with turbo-charged engines, counter-rotating propellers, and internal layouts. Models with tip-tanks somewhat resemble the Cessna 310, but 310 nacelles extend beyond trailing edge, 310 wing has no fairing between fuselage and nacelles, and 310 shows two windows on each side, including the pilot's.

Cessna 310, 320 Skyknight, U-3, L-27

Length: 29'7" (9.02 m)   *Wingspan:* 37'6" (11.43 m)   *Cruising speed:* variable, about 177 mph (285 km/h)

A variety of popular aircraft sharing the minimum characteristics of *twin engines on dihedral wing combined with level tail planes; very flat engine nacelles; tip-tanks; distinct point at the bottom of the tail fin.* Since 1969, there has also been a *noticeable ventral fin* (tail skid). Rare Skyknight has four small side windows. Close at hand, Cessna 310 and 320 tip-tanks are distinctly canted up and out from the wing.

Cessna's entry into the business twin market quickly became a military utility and liaison aircraft (U-3, L-27) and was produced continuously from 1954 to 1982. Model changes tended to emphasize minor changes in windows, streamlining, and engines. The 310s with ventral fin and without rear windows date from 1969 to 1973. The major change came in 1975, when the nose was lengthened and a turbocharged engine became available. The turbo versions cruise at more than 200 mph (322 km/h), and can be distinguished from the conventional engines by the absence of a cowl flap on the bottom of the nacelles.

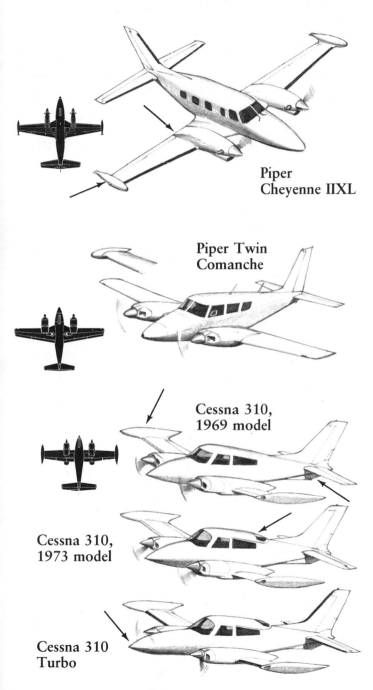

Piper
Cheyenne IIXL

Piper Twin
Comanche

Cessna 310,
1969 model

Cessna 310,
1973 model

Cessna 310
Turbo

Cessna 340, 335

Length: 34'4" (10.46 m)   *Wingspan:* 38'1" (11.62 m)   *Cruising speed:* 212 mph (341 km/h)

A *low-wing twin. Four small oval windows each side; noticeable ventral fin: long-fuselaged and short-nosed* in its general aspect; *engine nacelles extend past trailing edge, tip-tanks are canted outward at a 30-degree angle; dihedral in wing, none in tail plane.* Overhead, it could be confused with the smaller Cessna 310. These two Cessnas have straight leading edges on wings that arise directly from the fuselage without any fairing there, or at the engine nacelles, and have tip-tanks.

This four-passenger, two-crew, pressurized aircraft has flown since 1971. The model 335 is not pressurized, but has exactly the same window layout, giving no external evidence of its not being able to operate at 30,000 feet, as the 340 can.

Cessna 411, 414 and 421A, 421B Golden Eagle

421A specifications: *Length:* 33'9" (10.29 m)   *Wingspan:* 39'11" (12.17 m)   *Cruising speed:* 226 mph (364 km/h)

A series of similar twins. *Four or five passenger windows; tip-tanks; long noses, no ventral fin; strong dorsal fin fairing to highly swept tail fin.* All have the typical Cessna wing, straight leading edge, slight taper of trailing edge beginning at engine nacelles. *Dihedral in wing, none in tail plane.* Detail below main drawing shows the unpressurized model, the 411; note the single side window for the pilot (pressurized models have a two-part side window).

Still in production. Beginning in 1965, with the unpressurized Cessna 411, then in 1967, with pressurized versions, a series of six- to eight-passenger twins. The 414 is a less expensive, lower-powered version of the 421. Models built from 1965 to 1972 show four round windows. From 1973 to date, the 421 has had five oval passenger windows; the 414 added the fifth window in 1974.

Cessna 414A Chancellor and 421C Golden Eagle

Chancellor specifications: *Length:* 36'4" (11.04 m)   *Wingspan:* 44'1" (13.44 m); Golden Eagle, 41' (12.5 m)   *Cruising speed:* 211 mph (339 km/h)

A pair of similar turbocharged twin piston planes. *Five oval windows; dihedral in wing, none in tail plane; without tip-tanks.* Very similar 414 Chancellor and 421A, 421B Golden Eagle are identical, except *with* tip-tanks. Compare the almost identical Cessna Corsair, Conquest I, which has everything as in 414A and 421C, except for a very sharp dihedral in tail, and turboprop engines. That one company should make so many very similar models is curious, and an annoyance to the viewer.

Cessna created two new models by dropping the characteristic tip-tanks from its Golden Eagle and Chancellor series in 1976 (while continuing to manufacture planes with tip-tanks). The new models, designated 414A Chancellor and 421C Golden Eagle, offered slightly better performance and some greater ease in managing the fuel systems.

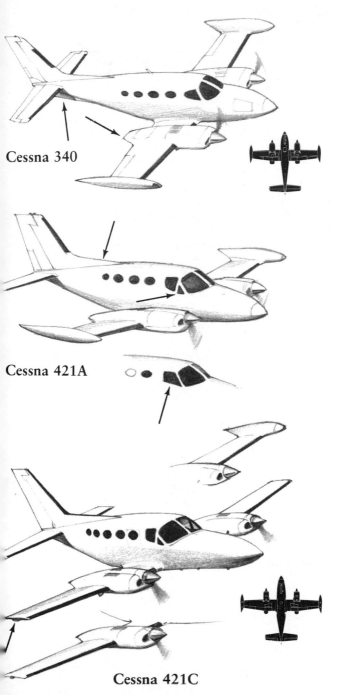

Cessna 340

Cessna 421A

Cessna 421C

Cessna 401, 402, Utiliner, Businessliner

Length: 36'1" (11 m) *Wingspan:* 39'10" (12.15 m) *Cruising speed:* 200 mph (322 km/h)

A *low-wing twin* with that Cessna look: *straight leading edge to wing; no fairing in wing at all; slight dihedral in wing, none in tail.* Models built from 1967 to 1971 (401, 402A, and early 402Bs) have four evenly spaced round windows that get smaller toward the tail. Models from 1971 on (later 402Bs and 402C) have five rectangular windows on each side, also tapering in size front to rear. All 402Bs have *tip-tanks* (see sketch).

Carrying a crew of one or two and six to nine passengers, Cessna Utiliners and Businessliners serve feeder lines and corporations. They aren't pressurized or particularly fast, but they're intended to be economical rather than exotic, as their sobriquets indicate.

Cessna 404 Titan

Length: 39'6" (12.04 m) *Wingspan:* 46'8" (14.23 m) *Cruising speed:* 230 mph (370 km/h)

A *low-wing twin. Very strong (12-degree) dihedral in tail.* Compare the Cessna Corsair and Conquest, which are turboprops. Titan has *shallow rectangular windows* compared to the Corsair's oval or the Conquest's almost square "TV screen" windows.

Largest of Cessna's unpressurized aircraft. Introduced in 1976, only a few hundred Titans were built in the next seven years. It was neither as fast as the Corsair it resembles in size nor as efficient as its smaller cousins, the 402 Businessliners and Utiliners.

Cessna 441 Conquest (now Conquest II) and Cessna 425 Corsair (now Conquest I)

441 Conquest specifications: *Length:* 39' (11.89 m) *Wingspan:* 49' (14.94 m) *Cruising speed:* 290 mph (467 km/h)

Both aircraft are *low-wing twin turboprops. Very strong (12-degree) dihedral in tail plane.* Except for the engine and the dihedral in the tail, the 425 Corsair (Conquest I) is identical to the Cessna 421C Golden Eagle. Corsairs are scarcer than DC3s. Overhead, a typical Cessna wing, unfaired at wing root or nacelles. Turboprop engines on the much more common 441 Conquest (Conquest II) extend far forward of the straight leading edge, and do not show past trailing edge. Corsair (Conquest I) is similar, but it shows nacelle behind. Except when directly overhead, the dihedral will be very noticeable.

Built since 1975, the Conquest was temporarily decertified because of problems with metal fatigue in the tail plane; since then, it's been remanufactured and strengthened. Carries eight to ten passengers and a crew of two. It can operate above 36,000 feet.

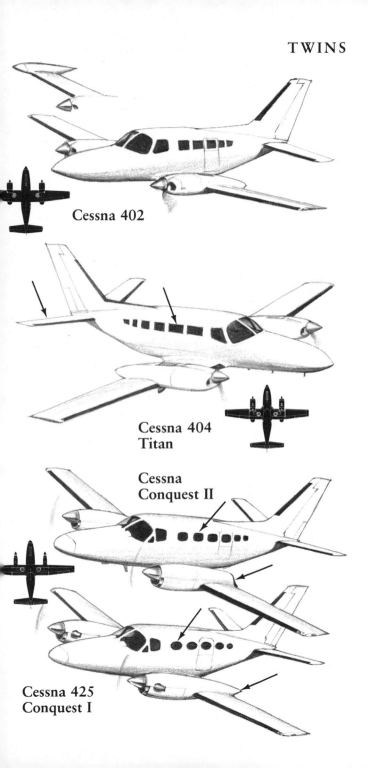

Cessna 402

Cessna 404
Titan

Cessna
Conquest II

Cessna 425
Conquest I

Beech Queen Air, U-8, U-21 Seminole

Length: 35'6" (10.82 m)   *Wingspan:* 45'10" (13.98 m)   *Cruising speed:* 230 mph (370 km/h)

A series of midsized *low-wing twins. Matching 7-degree dihedrals in wing and tail; strongly swept tail fin; three and four rectangular windows, port and starboard, with trailing small oval window. Earliest models (B65) had vertical tail fin.*

Beginning with the Queen Air 65 in 1958, a long series of successful small twins with various engines. The matching dihedral is typical of both the Queen Air and the conventional-tail King Air and is an unusual combination.

Beech King Air A90-E90, U-21, A100, B100

Model E90 (includes U.S. Army U-21) specifications: *Length:* 35'6" (10.32 m)   *Wingspan:* 50'3" (15.32 m)   *Cruising speed:* 260 mph (418 km/h)

A series of *low-winged, twin turboprops with conventional tail. Slight dihedral in wings and tail plane.* Typical Beech window details: *no window in passenger door,* one smaller window bringing up the rear, *after a blank spot.* Stretched A100 is 4 feet longer than other models; has six large and one small window, starboard; and five large and one small, port side. Others models show four large windows, one small on starboard; three large, one small on port.

More than 1000 King Airs in service, the stretched A100 is a common feeder line 12-passenger plane. The other versions are six-passenger. Early King Airs were essentially pressurized Queen Airs with turboprop engines; easily distinguished overhead by the engine noise, on the ground by the round pressurized windows fitted in the same pattern as the Queen Air's square passenger windows.

Beech Super King Air B200, T-44, U-12

Length: 43'9" (13.16 m)   *Wingspan:* 54'6" (16.6 m)   *Cruising speed:* 320 mph (515 km/h)

A *low-winged twin turboprop with a T-tail.* Compare Piper Cheyenne III. *Round passenger windows,* last one always smaller. *Optional tip-tanks* are commonly seen.

Developed in 1969, the Super King Air took the conventional King Air, increased the wing span, upped the engine power, and added the T-tail. Earliest Super King Airs show four large round windows each side; later models show five on the port side, six on the starboard, plus the small last window on both sides. A U.S. Navy trainer as T-44, a U.S. Army, Navy, and Air Force transport and VIP as C-12 and UC-12.

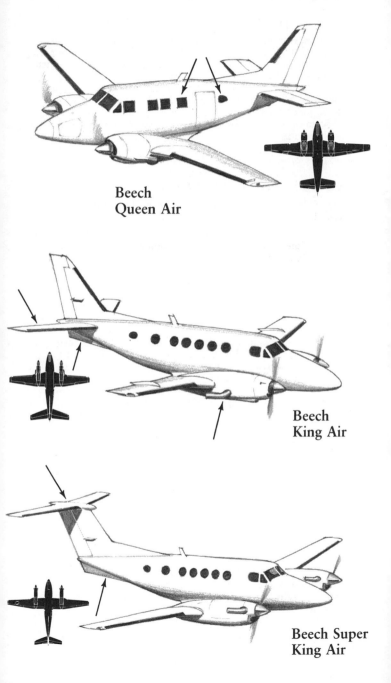

Beech
Queen Air

Beech
King Air

Beech Super
King Air

Piper PA42 Cheyenne III, IV

Length: 43'5" (12.24 m)   *Wingspan:* 47'8" (14.53 m)   *Cruising speed:* 318 mph (512 km/h)

A *business-size, low-wing twin turboprop with a T-tail, tip-tanks, and rectangular windows. Typical Piper wing, strong fairing wing root to nacelle.* (Compare the Beech Super King Air, which has optional tip-tanks and round windows.)

Operational since 1980, an exceptionally fast turboprop business plane: One circled the world in 1982 in 88 hours of flying time with 13 stops for fuel and rest. Seats six in comfort—or up to 11 in discomfort—plus a crew of two. The Cheyenne IV, scheduled to be delivered in 1984, will be virtually identical, but new turboprop engines will have nacelles that *do not* extend beyond the trailing edge.

Cessna Skymaster, 337 O-2

Length: 29'9" (9.07 m)   *Wingspan:* 38'2" (11.63 m)   *Cruising speed:* 173 mph (278 km/h)

Fairly common. One of two *twin-boom* airplanes in military use. (Compare the OV-10, page 166.) Combination of twin boom and *one pusher, one puller propellers* is absolutely diagnostic. Pressurized version (bottom sketch) has much smaller side windows.

The civilian version was successful; more than 1400 model 337s fly in the U.S. and Canada. The idea was that in the case of the failure of one engine, the plane would not suffer the sudden and consistent pull by the remaining engine. Cessna hoped the plane would be a twin that could be operated on a single-engine pilot rating. The government quashed that idea, and the Skymaster was dropped by Cessna in the U.S. in 1980. Still manufactured in France, by a Cessna subsidiary, as the Reims Milirole. Some 400 in U.S. military service. A nonretractable model 336 is very rare.

Mitsubishi MU2 Marquise, Solitaire

Marquise specifications: *Length:* 39'5" (12.01 m)   *Wingspan:* 39'2" (11.94 m)   *Cruising speed:* Marquise, 340 mph (547 km/h); Solitaire, 370 mph (595 km/h)

A fairly common, *small, high-wing twin turboprop. Tip-tanks; tail plane set noticeably lower than wings.* Earlier Japanese-built *Marquise has bulging fuselage fairings to hold retractable wheels.* American-assembled *Solitaire has smooth fuselage into which gear retracts.* Early Japanese Marquise models are 33 feet long; all American Solitaires are also 33 feet.

An increasingly popular corporate plane. The relatively high cruising speed, combined with fuel efficiency and room for four to nine passengers, made it the hot-rod of twin turbos. It even became a popular plane to steal and use in the Caribbean drug-smuggling underground. Several models (the plane comes with a variety of engines) have ranges up to 1680 miles (2700 km), which is long for the class.

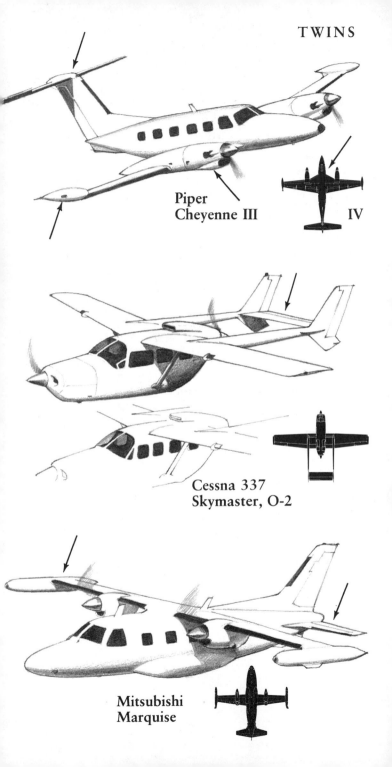

TWINS

Piper
Cheyenne III   IV

Cessna 337
Skymaster, O-2

Mitsubishi
Marquise

Gulfstream and Rockwell Commander, Shrike Commander, Aero Commander, etc.

Aero Commander 520 specifications: *Length:* 34'6" (10.52 m)
Wingspan: 44'7" (13.60 m)   *Cruising speed:* 197 mph (317 km/h)
Turbo Commander 690 specifications: *Length:* 44'4" (13.51 m)
Wingspan: 46'8" (14.22 m)   *Cruising speed:* 288 mph (463 km/h)
Shrike Commander (Aero Commander 500U) specifications:
Length: 35'1" (10.69 m)   *Wingspan:* 49'2" (15 m)   *Cruising speed:* 201 mph (323 km/h)

A complex family of airplanes. Began in 1948 with the four-passenger piston-engine Aero Commander and proceeded through the turboprop Rockwell 690 and Gulfstream 840, 900, 980 and 1000 series, carrying as many as ten passengers. All share certain characteristics: *high wing with slight dihedral, twin engines, strong dihedral in tail planes.* Models with turboprops from 690B on have small winglets. Very earliest four-passenger Aero Commanders and Shrike Commanders have a curved leading edge to the tail fin; all later models, a straight-edged, strongly swept tail fin. Another characteristic, from the Aero Commander on, is the *upswept fuselage,* which becomes increasingly distinct as the later models appear. Gulfstream will continue to produce 840, 900, and 1000 airframes, seating seven to ten passengers. Long-nosed and streamlined, compared to other high-wing twins. The streamlining effect is visually enhanced by the dihedrals in wing and tail plane. The authors accept the judgment of other airplane aficionados who lump the whole, varied, 25-year-old class of airplanes under the single category: Commanders.

de Havilland DHC6 Twin Otter

Length: 51'9" (15.77 m)   *Wingspan:* 65' (19.81 m)   *Cruising speed:* 200 mph (322 km/h)

Slim-bodied, with *long, thin high wings* and *twin turboprops; fixed gear; conventional tail; wing braced from fuselage at landing gear root.* Compare somewhat similar and much rarer G.A.F. Nomad (page 118), whose wing brace rises from the landing gear itself.

Built since 1965, it's one of the most popular small airline and air-taxi planes ever built. More than 800 are in service and it is still in production. Carries 14 to 18 passengers in a fairly quiet, center-aisle cabin. Very short takeoff and landing qualities; can take off across the width of most airports. Seen as a float plane, though not as often as the de Havilland single-engine Otter.

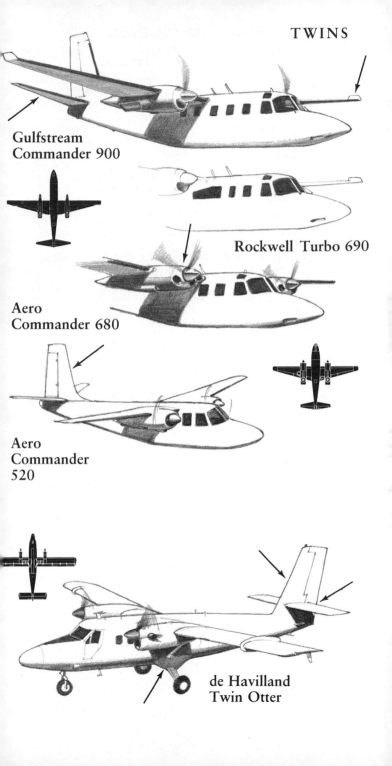

TWINS

Gulfstream
Commander 900

Rockwell Turbo 690

Aero
Commander 680

Aero
Commander
520

de Havilland
Twin Otter

Britten-Norman Islander, Trislander

Islander specifications: *Length:* 35'8" (10.87 m) *Wingspan:* 49'
(14.94 m) *Cruising speed:* 150 mph (241 km/h)

A plane of odd geometry. *Fuselage rectangular in cross section; varied window shapes,* rectangular, trapezoidal, rhomboid; *Hershey-bar wing and tail; curved wing tips* are auxiliary fuel tanks; *double wheels* on *lumpy nonretractable landing gear.*

Designed for fuel-efficient, low-speed, low-density commuter routes. More than 1000 Islanders have been delivered worldwide since 1967. The earlier versions had a short nose; whereas the last version, the Trislander, has a longer fuselage, a T-tail, and a third engine mounted high on the tail fin. A low-technology airplane, it has been manufactured under license in Romania and assembled from supplied parts in the Philippines. Seats up to 18 passengers and a single pilot; no aisle, entry through doors directly to seats.

CASA C212 Aviocar

Length: 49'10" (15.2 m) *Wingspan:* 62'4" (19 m) *Cruising speed:* 196 mph (315 km/h)

Still rare. *Stubby look, high wings, twin turboprops, upswept rear fuselage, conventional tail, nonretractable gear.* Compare equally stubby Shorts Skyvan, which has braced wing and unswept fuselage, or de Havilland Dash 8, which is upswept but has T-tail and retractable gear.

CASA is Spain's aircraft manufacturer, and the Aviocar is their design. Originally, a 16-man paratroop transport and utility freighter or air ambulance. The civil versions can carry 19 passengers and operate from the shortest and roughest of airstrips. A popular commuter aircraft in the Far East and African countries, where it replaces the aging WWII-surplus planes that have ended their careers in Third World airlines.

Israel Aircraft Industries Arava 101B
Cargo Commuterliner

Length: 42'9" (13.03 m) *Wingspan:* 68'9" (20.96 m) *Cruising speed:* 193 mph (311 km/h)

Introduced into the U.S. in 1982. *Very long, thin, constant-chord wings; bathtub body; and twin booms to double tail fin.* The only possible confusion is Cessna's twin-boom Skymaster (page 110) if all one looked at was the twin boom—the airplanes are otherwise totally different in shape and size.

Developed in Israel as a military transport in 1972; civilian version certified in the U.S. in 1980. Purchased by several small airlines in 1982. Seats up to 20, plus a crew of one or two. The use of long, thin wings combined with fixed gear and tubby fuselages is characteristic of the 1970s. The high-lift advantage of the ribbon wing was known from sailplane technology, but it required space-age materials to make a ribbon wing strong enough to support a small airliner.

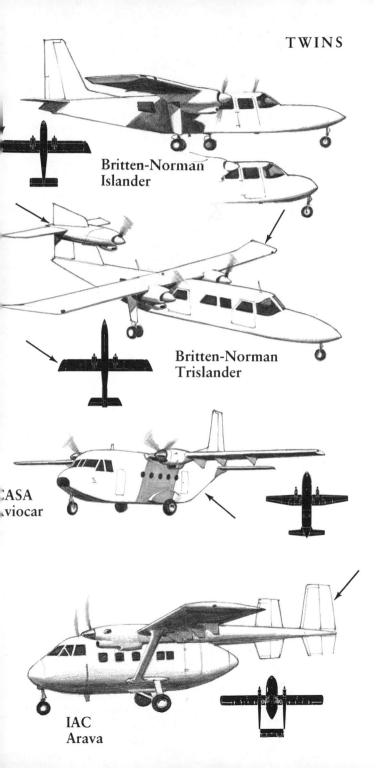

TWINS

Britten-Norman
Islander

Britten-Norman
Trislander

CASA
Aviocar

IAC
Arava

Shorts Skyliner, Skyvan

Length: 40'1" (12.22 m)   *Wingspan:* 64'11" (19.79 m)   *Cruising speed:* 173 mph (278 km/h)

Stubby, fixed landing gear with wheels tucked up under body; twin tail fins; long, thin wings with braces.

Resembling a flying bathtub with a thin wing glued on the top, the Short Brothers Skyvans serve small airlines in eastern North America and Alaska. The plane, built of a metal-resin composite with little or no insulation, seems remarkably noisy to passengers who took to flying after the DC3 era. More than 150 Skyvans (or more luxuriously appointed Skyliners) were built from 1964 to 1982.

Shorts 330, Sherpa 360

Length: 58' (17.69 m)   *Wingspan:* 74'8" (22.67 m)   *Cruising speed:* 173 mph (278 km/h)

Bizarre configuration: *long, thin, untapered wing with large strut; semiretractable wheels* show even in flight. Most models have a *double tail fin,* like their brother, the Shorts Skyvan (above). One is not surprised that the builder, Short Brothers Company, was once a leading manufacturer of flying boats.

Introduced in 1976 as a fuel-efficient feeder airliner, the 30-seat Shorts 330 is of composite metal and resin construction; very light weight and low maintenance. A slightly larger version, the Shorts 360, carrying 36 passengers and bearing a conventional tail, has been purchased by several North American commuter airlines. A variant 330 will appear in the U.S. Air Force by 1985.

de Havilland DHC8 Dash 8

Length: 75'6" (23.01 m)   *Wingspan:* 84' (25.6 m)   *Cruising speed:* 280 mph (451 km/h)

Rare. Just coming into production: *twin turboprops that extend well before and behind a high wing; upswept rear fuselage combined with T-tail, retractable landing gear.*

A little brother (32 passengers) of de Havilland's successful four-engined Dash 7. Slight dihedral in the wings, combined with the wide-span tail plane, gives the Dash 8 some of the elegance of the Dash 7. It is being designed with slow-rotation, four-bladed propellers and new turbo engines to operate as quietly as possible from urban airports.

Fokker, Fairchild Hiller, F27 Mk 500

Length: 82'2" (25 m)   *Wingspan:* 95'2" (29 m)   *Cruising speed:* 298 mph (479 km/h)

Fairly common, largest of the high-wing airliners; *12 oval windows, heavy tail fairing parallels slight upsweep of the lower fuselage; very pointy nosed with prominent, long engine nacelles.*

Still built in Holland; U.S. production by Fairchild ended in 1966. The Mk 500 is by far the most common model, plus a few of the original F27s (length: 77'4") and a variant, the FH227 (length: 83'8"). Although not numerous (fewer than 80 in service in 1984), the Fokker F27 has always been highly visible as a feeder airliner into major airports.

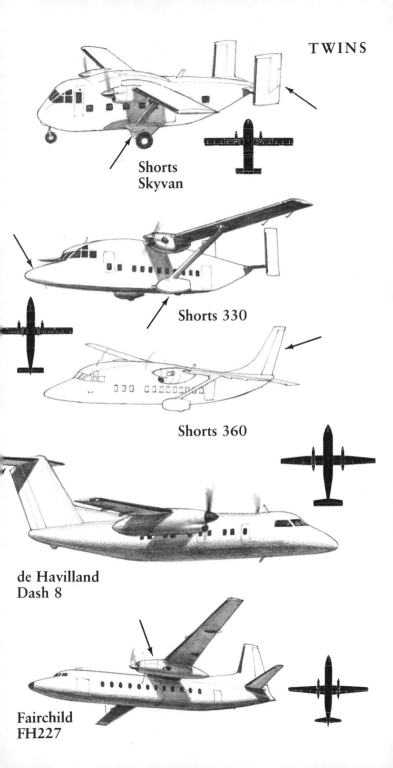

TWINS

Shorts
Skyvan

Shorts 330

Shorts 360

de Havilland
Dash 8

Fairchild
FH227

Aerospatiale (Nord) 262, Mohawk 298

Length: 63'3" (19.28 m) *Wingspan:* 71'10" (21.90 m) *Cruising speed:* 233 mph (375 km/h)

Rare, local. *High, thin, tapering wings; bulging landing gear nacelles on fuselage; tires exposed even when retracted.*
This 26-passenger short-haul airliner went into service in 1963 and, with improved engines, has survived into the 1980s. It was one of the first of the high-efficiency, short-distance airliners, and was soon surpassed by later models (the Shorts 300, for example). Only 110 were built; perhaps a dozen still carry passengers.

GAF (Government Aircraft Factory, Australia) Nomad

Length: 41'2" (12.56 m); long-nosed model N24, 47'1" (14.36 m) *Wingspan:* 54'2" (16.51 m) *Cruising speed:* 193 mph (311 km/h)

Rare, but increasing in North America. *High wing, twin turboprops; tail plane mounted partway up tail fin; wing struts rise out of the wheel pants of the fixed landing gear* (compare the de Havilland Twin Otter strut and tail).
Developed by the Australian factory as a military search and rescue and light transport in 1971. Two civil versions: the short-nosed N22 for 12 passengers, the long-nosed N24 for 15. Competitive in the same market as the DHC Twin Otter and, as such, may be seen fitted with floats. Several have been ordered by North American air taxis and commuter airlines.

Handley Page and British Aerospace Jetstream 31

Length: 47'1" (14.35 m) *Wingspan:* 52' (15.85 m) *Cruising speed:* 269 mph (433 km/h)

Not common. Combines *low wing, turboprops, unswept tail plane mounted well up on tail fin, modest fairing to tail fin, and seven small round windows on each side.* Newest version, the BAe Jetstream 31, has a *distinct ventral fin.* Compare the Merlin IVA, with distinct dorsal fin/tail fairing, of which some early models had ten small round windows.
The venerable Handley Page Company went broke in 1970 after designing and building the prototype of the successful Jetstream. It is now built by the Scottish division of British Aerospace. Handley Page types (illustrated) show a much longer propeller spinner than the current production model 31, with Garrett turboprops. Each carries 18 passengers.

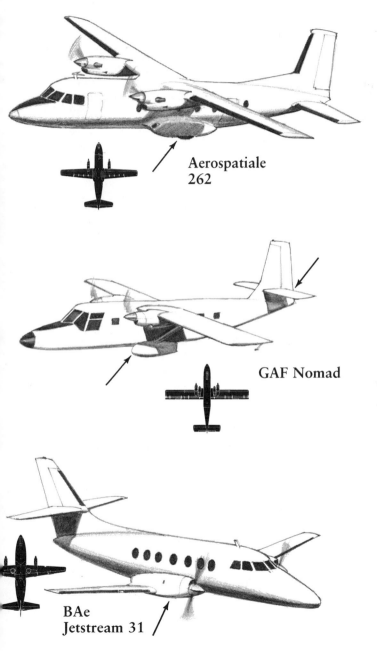

Aerospatiale
262

GAF Nomad

BAe
Jetstream 31

Swearingen (now Fairchild) Merlin II

Length: 40'1" (12.22 m)   *Wingspan:* 45'11" (14 m)   *Cruising speed:* 295 mph (475 km/h)

Small and fairly common. *Low wing, conventional tail, turboprops.* Resembles a smoother, bulkier, more streamlined Beech Queen Air. *Three rather large rectangular windows on each side.*

Swearingen, a company that specialized in putting turboprops, streamlined fairings and pressurization into other companies' production aircraft, took the Queen Air wing and built a streamlined, pressurized fuselage for it from scratch. The small number of fairly large windows is unusual in a pressurized aircraft. Compare the Beech King Air (five or six small windows) or the Cessna Conquest (six small windows) for conventional treatment of similarly sized aircraft.

Swearingen (Fairchild) Merlin III, Fairchild 300

Length: 42'2" (12.85 m)   *Wingspan:* 46'3" (14.10 m)   *Cruising speed:* 288 mph (463 km/h)

Common. Combines *low symmetrically tapering wing* with *strongly swept tail plane mounted midway up and well forward on the tail fairing.* Compare larger Merlin IV (next entry). Similarly configured Handley Page Jetstream 31 has unswept tail plane mounted farther back on the fin and shows seven small round windows. The midtailed Rockwell Commander 700 has trapezoidal windows, unswept tail plane and, unlike the Merlin or the Jetstream, has no ventral fin at all.

A popular series of executive turboprops. Some early Merlin IIIs have only three or four windows to a side, and a variety of turboprop engines have been mounted on the same basic airframe. The strong dorsal and ventral fins shown on the Merlin and the Handley Page Jetstream are intended to improve handling when the plane is forced to fly on one engine. The 1984 Fairchild 300 has winglets.

Fairchild Merlin IVA, Metro III, Fairchild 400

Length: 59'4" (18.08 m)   *Wingspan:* 46'3" (14.10 m)   *Cruising speed:* 279 mph (449 km/h)

Common. Combines *low, symmetrically tapered wings and strongly swept tail plane mounted well forward on the tail fin fairing.* Compare the smaller Merlin IIIB (previous entry).

Carrying 12 passengers in the Merlin IVA executive cabin or up to 20 passengers in the Metro airliner cabin, this Swearingen-designed airplane has seen some use in the U.S. Midwest as a commuter airliner. It is quite rare as an executive plane. Some 300 delivered worldwide since 1971. Swearingen, now a division of Fairchild, began as a converter of other companies' aircraft to corporate executive planes. The 1983 models introduced winglets; the Merlin IVA was renamed Fairchild 400 in 1984.

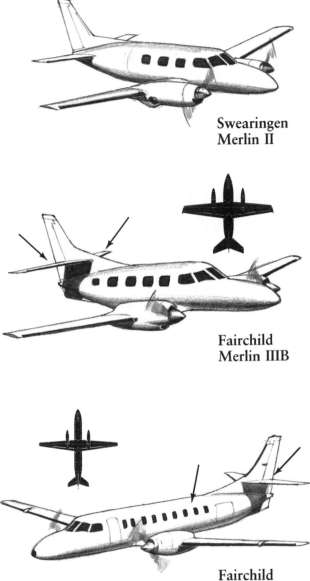

Swearingen
Merlin II

Fairchild
Merlin IIIB

Fairchild
Metro III

Beech 99 Airliner

Length: 44'7" (13.59 m)   *Wingspan:* 45'10" (13.97 m)   *Cruising speed:* 270 mph (434 km/h)

A common and variable aircraft. Combines *low wing with two turboprop engines, conventional tail, and distinct ventral fin.* Unfortunately, it has to be distinguished from similar planes, including its predecessor, the Beech Queen Air, by *noting the window patterns.* The 99s show, from the front, one small rectangular window; five or six larger rectangular windows; the typical Beech gap on or opposite the passenger door; and a small oval window at the rear.

There are a couple of hundred of the 15-passenger stretched and pressurized version of the Beech Queen Air in service with dozens of small airlines. Built since 1965, with a couple of engine variations. A rather ordinary-looking aircraft, with a moderately swept tail fin (compared to the Queen Air) and a long, pointy nose.

Embraer EMB110 Bandeirante

Length: 47'10" (14.58 m)   *Wingspan:* 50'3" (15.32 m)   *Cruising speed:* 203 mph (327 km/h)

An increasingly common commuter airliner. *Low-winged; twin turboprops;* in the air, *a strong impression of rectangularity: Note the sharp extension of the tail fin down through the tail plane to a ventral fin; overhead, slightly tapering wing and tail planes look quite rectangular; engines with deep nacelles* (to hold landing gear) *extend very far forward of the wing.* The wraparound *cockpit windows are composed of eight separate panes,* which is most unusual in recently built aircraft. The 1984 model has a dihedral in tailplane.

A 17- to 19-passenger unpressurized aircraft first delivered to the U.S. in 1976. The Bandeirante competes directly with such small commuter airliners as the Beech 99. The parent company, Empresa Brasilia de Aeronautica, builds single- and twin-engine Piper airplanes under license; it also manufactures components for Northrop's F-5 fighters.

Embraer EMB120 Brasilia

Length: 64'5" (19.64 m)   *Wingspan:* 74'10" (19.76 m)   *Cruising speed:* 288 mph (463 km/h)

A 1984 introduction. *Very large low-wing twin turboprop* with *T-tail* (of twin T-tails, compare the much smaller Piper Seminole, Duchess, Cheyenne III, and Beech Super King Air). The only other large twin T-tail is the *high-winged* de Havilland DHC8 Dash 8. High overhead, they might be confused if you do not pay attention to the wing placement.

Ordered by commuter airlines from coast to coast, this 30-passenger airliner includes state-of-the-art technology. The fuel-efficient Canadian-built turboprops have an unusual feature: fully disengageable propellers, so that the engines can be run at the loading gate. This feature allows passengers to load while keeping the air-conditioning and heating systems on, as it does getting back in the air without the delays associated with engine starting.

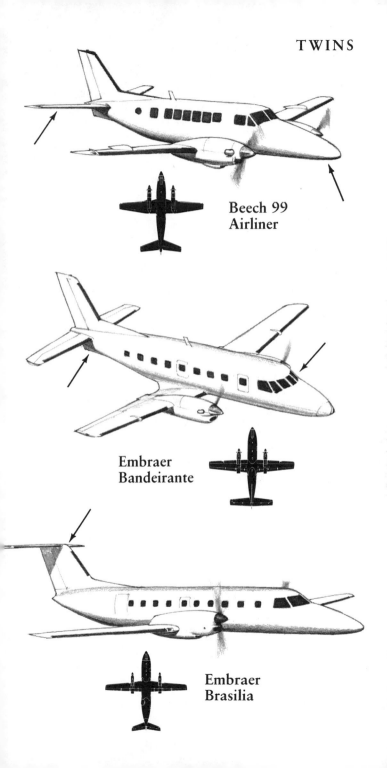

Beech 99
Airliner

Embraer
Bandeirante

Embraer
Brasilia

Beechcraft 1900 Airliner

Length: 57'9" (17.60 m)   *Wingspan:* 54'6" (16.61 m)   *Cruising speed:* 280 mph (451 km/h)

New, not yet common. Combines *low wing with T-tail, fuselage-mounted winglets just forward of tail;* typical Beech wing begins with *rectangular section from fuselage to engine; trailing edge tapers to tip more sharply than leading edge.*

A 19-passenger aircraft intended for commuter routes requiring frequent stops; it is just beginning to appear on the flight line. The sharp dihedral in the low wing, combined with the T-tail, gives the 1900 a unique appearance in the landing and takeoff pattern. Note also the very large double engine exhausts.

British Aerospace 748

Length: 67' (20.42 m)   *Wingspan:* 102'5" (31.22 m)   *Cruising speed:* 281 mph (452 km/h)

One of two modern *twin turboprops.* Compare the Japanese NAMC YS11, which shares the characteristic of *massive bulge on bottom of engine nacelle* (houses landing gear). The BAe 748 has *strong wing dihedral, beginning at fuselage* (compare the Martin 404, whose dihedral begins at engines), combined with *horizontal tail planes.* Convair 640 has similar wing and tail configuration but without the massive landing gear fairings. Passenger BAe 748s have ten large rounded windows. The NAMC has many small, square windows.

There are certain realities that jet aircraft did not make go away; for instance, the need for fuel-efficient, conventional aircraft. Even the Queen of England has two BAe 748s at her disposal. It seats 44 passengers, and the specific market it sought was as a replacement for aging Douglas DC3s. A few are operated by U.S. and Canadian feeder airlines.

Saab-Fairchild 340 Commuter

Length: 63'9" (19.43 m)   *Wingspan:* 70'4" (21.44 m)   *Cruising speed:* estimated, 300 mph (483 km/h)

New, expected in air by 1984. A fairly conventional-looking airplane: *Tall, swept tail fin, strongly dihedral tail plane; deep fuselage is carried full depth well aft; unusual engine nacelles, which are narrow and deep, rise high above and show well below wing.*

A 34-passenger airliner with wings and tail by Fairchild, the rest by Saab; it's to be assembled in Sweden. We have not seen it fly, but we expect that the aspect of the plane will be unique—strong dihedrals in tail planes tend to be unusually noticeable, as on the Martin 404. The bulky body and slim wing will attract attention, as that combination does now in, for example, the Shorts 360.

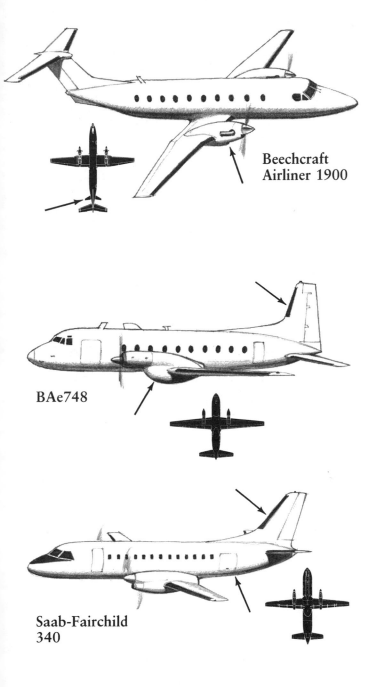

Beechcraft
Airliner 1900

BAe748

Saab-Fairchild
340

Grumman American G159 Gulfstream I

Length: 64'8" (19.72 m)   *Wingspan:* 78'4" (23.88 m)   *Cruising speed:* 288 mph (463 km/h)

Not common. *Slim-winged; short-nosed; distinct swelling under engine nacelles* houses landing gear. A stretched version, the G159 1C, is 10 feet longer and shows seven, rather than five, oval passenger windows.

Carrying 24 passengers in the short version, or 37 in the model 1C stretch, some 200 of these durable, but not particularly fuel-efficient, corporate planes operate in North America. Though built from 1960, with the stretching done in the early 1980s, they're not currently competitive with newer aircraft of the same capacity.

Martin 404

Length: 74'7" (22.73 m)   *Wingspan:* 93'3" (28.42 m)   *Cruising speed:* 280 mph (451 km/h)

A rare and handsome classic. Of the many old and new *twin-engine, low-wing* airliners, only the Martin shows a *distinct dihedral in the wing, beginning at the engines,* and a clearly *dihedral tail plane.*

Built from 1947 to 1953, only a handful of 404s fly today. The dihedral wing and tail plane turns the head of anyone who thinks it's just another Convair 240 series. The plane has not been refitted with turboprops like so many of its contemporaries, so it still has a satisfying, attention-getting roar to it.

Convair CV240, 340, 440, 540, 580, 600, 640

CV580 specifications: *Length:* 81'6" (24.84 m)   *Wingspan:* 105'4" (32.11 m)   *Cruising speed:* 300 mph (483 km/h)

A variety of highly similar *twin-engine, low-wing* airliners, with *slight dihedral in wing, and horizontal tail planes.* In the U.S. and Canada, most are *turboprop conversions,* series 540 to 640. (CV580 is the most common.) Except for the engine nacelles, very similar to the BAe HS748 and NAMC YS11. Whether old piston or new turboprop, *the nacelles are slim* compared to the bulging, landing-gear-holding nacelles on the HS748 and YS11.

The original 240, 340, 440 series, seating 40 to 50 passengers, with Pratt and Whitney radials, have been supplanted for the most part by turboprop conversions. A few made-from-scratch turboprops produced by Canadair—the Canadair CC-109—are still in service as troop carriers in the Canadian armed forces. Model numbers reflect little except the time of manufacture or re-engining. However, the 340 and 440 were slightly stretched versions of the original 240.

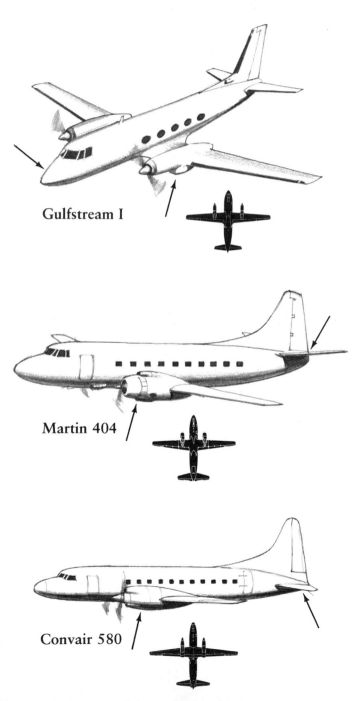

Gulfstream I

Martin 404

Convair 580

NAMC YS11

Length: 86'3" (26.30 m)   *Wingspan:* 104'11" (32 m)   *Cruising speed:* 281 mph (452 km/h)

Not common, but seen especially in Alaska and in the southwestern U.S. *Massive landing gear fairings under nacelles* (compare the BAe 748), *slight dihedral wing; horizontal tail plane; dozens of tiny, rectangular windows.*

Either the limits of conventional airplane design were reached in the 1950s or this is a virtual copy of the British Aerospace 748. Its design was begun in 1960, a year after the 748 went to the drawing board. The YS11 does carry 60 passengers, not 44, but is otherwise highly similar to the BAe 748; the windows are the most obvious difference.

Curtiss C-46

Length: 76'4" (23.27 m)   *Wingspan:* 108' (32.92 m)   *Cruising speed:* 235 mph (378 km/h)

A rare survivor. (Make sure it's not a DC3 before deciding.) *The plane with no nose; greenhouse cockpit windows;* the wings are like the DC3's, strongly tapered on the leading edge, straight on the trailing edge. Unlike the DC3, has *fully retractable landing gear.*

Developed as a 36-passenger airliner in 1940 to compete with the DC3, it was built as only a military transport. A few dozen still survive with small, poor regional airlines; likeliest to be seen in the Caribbean, southwestern Alaska, along the Mexican border. It's not nearly so common as the somewhat similar DC3.

Douglas DC3, C-47, Dakota

Length: 64'5" (19.65 m)   *Wingspan:* 95' (28.96 m)   *Cruising speed:* 194 mph (312 km/h)

Not common, but widely distributed. A *tail-dragger* that sits nose up on the flight line; in the air, *very short-nosed look,* as the wings are set well forward and the large radials flank the cockpit area; wing tapers on the leading edge only; *tires of forward landing gear do not retract out of sight; tail wheel is nonretractable.*

First built in 1935 and flown the world over, with several hundred surviving long after the assembly shut down in 1946. Seated 36 in unpressurized discomfort, as many as 50 in its troop-carrying configuration. Still flying passengers in all parts of North America, with hundreds parked on airfields and making occasional unscheduled freight trips. A few still in government service in Canada. As with many aircraft with partially retractable wheels, the purpose is to allow for a relatively safe landing in the event that the gear is not, or cannot be, lowered.

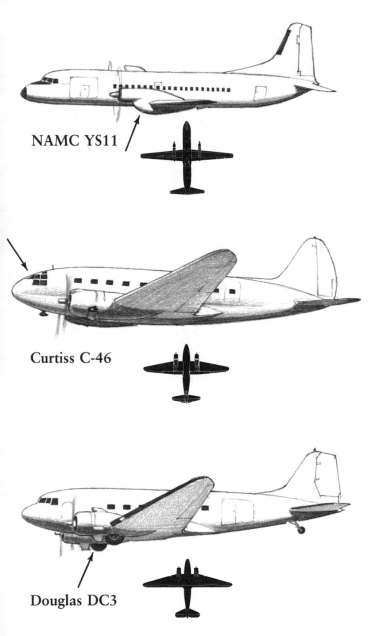

NAMC YS11

Curtiss C-46

Douglas DC3

de Havilland DH104 Dove, Riley Turbo-Exec Dove

Length: 39'4" (12 m)   *Wingspan:* 57' (17.37 m)   *Cruising speed:* 162 mph (261 km/h)

Increasingly rare. *Long, tapering wings; engines mounted well forward on the wing; distinctive bump over cockpit* gives crew stand-up headroom. Originals show a conventional curved tail, whereas Riley turbo-charged conversions have a swept, angular tail fin.

About 600 built by de Havilland between 1946 and 1968, many as military light transports. They became a popular executive aircraft after WWII, and the turbo conversions continue to fly in general aviation. A Dove with the old Gipsy Queen engines is a real rarity in North America.

Beech 18, C-45

Length: 35'2" (10.72 m)   *Wingspan:* 49'8" (15.14 m)   *Cruising speed:* 185 mph (298 km/h)

Still common, but highly variable. Twin-engine, low-wing, *distinctive Beech twin tail:* Note that *tail plane does not extend through fins.* Seen with rounded (early) and squared-off (late model) wing tips.

The durable Beech 18 was built from 1937 to 1972, with thousands in WWII as C-45s. It has been refitted in a bewildering variety of forms: with tricycle gear to replace the semiretractable tail-dragging gear; in stretched versions; in long-nosed models; with turboprop engines; with conventional rather than double-fin tails; and in one bizarre case, with a T-tail. *The odd window pattern—a long, rectangular passenger window surrounded by two smaller square windows—is always a good field mark.* The last production 18s were sold to Japan Airlines.

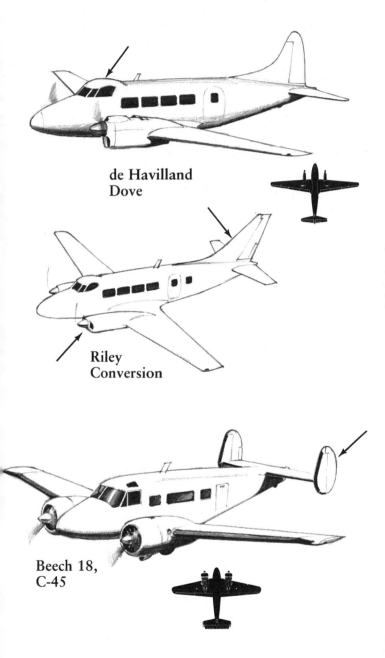

de Havilland
Dove

Riley
Conversion

Beech 18,
C-45

Lockheed 10, and 12 "Electra Jr."

Model 12 specifications: *Length:* 36'4" (11.07 m) *Wingspan:* 49'6" (15.09 m) *Cruising speed:* 206 mph (331 km/h)

Very rare. These are similar, but the model 10 has five side windows; the model 12, three. *Twin radial engines on low-wing, classic double-fin Lockheed tail; tail plane extends through the fin; main landing gear quite visible when retracted into open wheel wells.*

The model 10, first flown in 1934, was America's first all-metal-skin airplane. Quickly adopted by airlines, it carried 12 passengers and a crew of two. The smaller "Electra, Jr." model 12, carrying six passengers and a crew of two, was intended for the corporate plane and feeder airline business. Though only a couple of dozen 12s and not more than 5 model 10s are flying, we could not exclude these grandparents of a famous family of propeller airliners, culminating in the Super Constellation.

Lockheed L18 Lodestar, C-60

Length: 49'10" (15.37 m) *Wingspan:* 65'6" (20.21 m) *Cruising speed:* 229 mph (368 km/h)

Rare and worth looking for. *Wing mounted just below midpoint of fuselage; twin tail; tail plane extends through tail fins; two radial engines.* The more common Beech 18 is much smaller, and does not have the Lockheed-type tail planes extending through the vertical fins.

The premier short-haul airliner just as World War II started and a common personnel carrier (C-60) through the war. A distinctly tail-dragging aircraft with the nose pointed up as if it should be flying, it's usually seen sitting idle on a runway apron. Carried 14 passengers in relative comfort, including a full lavatory in the rear of the aircraft.

Cessna Bobcat, Crane T-50, AT-8, C-78

Length: 32'9" (10 m) *Wingspan:* 41'11" (12.8 m) *Cruising speed:* 165 mph (265 km/h)

Rare, small, and old-fashioned-looking twin, with *huge radials compared to the size of the plane; long-nosed, but the nose barely extends past the engine nacelles; partially retractable landing gear.*

Built by the thousands from 1940 to 1945 as a primary (T-50) and advanced (AT-8) multiengine trainer for the U.S. (Bobcat) and Canadian (Crane) armed forces. Several hundred served as light transports (C-78). Many converted to civil air after WWII, but wooden wings did not allow conversion to more efficient turboprops. Slightly underpowered, they're not really flyable on one engine; nevertheless, a durable, reliable short-haul aircraft.

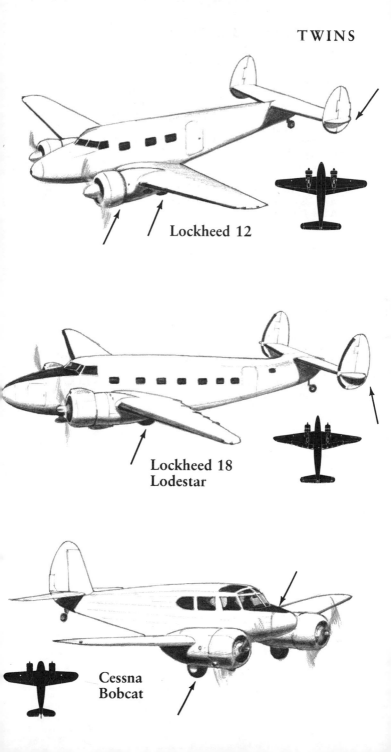

TWINS

Lockheed 12

Lockheed 18
Lodestar

Cessna
Bobcat

North American B-25 Mitchell

Length: 52'11" (16.33 m)   *Wingspan:* 67'7" (20.86 m)   *Cruising speed:* 250 mph (402 km/h)

Rare, variable. Combines *midwing with double tail fins*. Note that it is a "high" midwing, and the tail plane does not extend through the vertical fins. Compare the somewhat similar Lockheed Lodestar, with its much lower wing mounting and tail plane extending through the twin tail fins.

Designed before World War II, more than 10,000 were built; losses kept the inventory to about 2600 maximum during WWII. Produced with and without the glass bombardier's nose; civil conversions usually have closed-in noses and some will have tip-tanks; a few have passenger windows. Once fairly popular as an aerial sprayer. Carrier-launched B-25s made the token attack on Tokyo in April 1942; B-25s were the aircraft seen in the 1970s movie *Catch-22*.

Douglas A-26, B-26 Invader

Length: 53'10" (16.40 m)   *Wingspan:* 70' (21.34 m)   *Cruising speed:* 325 mph (523 km/h)

Rare, variable. Look for the constants. *Wing mounted very high, but not above fuselage; two huge, cylindrical engine nacelles that extend well forward and back of the wing; nacelles mounted low on wing; long bulging nose; shallow cockpit windows.*

Once you get the configuration, you can ignore the dozens of variations of the basic aircraft: As a high-speed, large-capacity executive conversion, you may run across B-26s with completely enclosed noses, with passenger windows, and with tip-tanks on the wings, but the basic wing and engine conformation is undisturbed and unmistakable. Known as the A-26 (for attack bomber) through WWII, but redesignated B-26 after the war—which gives you a chance to listen for an anachronism while watching war movies. The WWII B-26 was the Martin Marauder, with short, tapering engine nacelles.

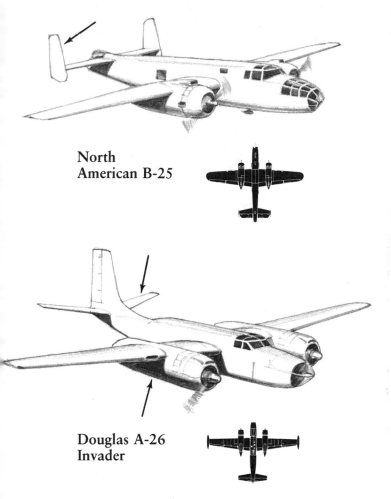

North
American B-25

Douglas A-26
Invader

de Havilland Dash 7

Length: 80'8" (24.58 m)   *Wingspan:* 93' (28.35 m)   *Cruising speed:* 235 mph (378 km/h) Mach 0.354

Common. The only *four-engine, high-wing, T-tail* commercial aircraft in North America. Even when seen directly overhead, when it might be confused with the high-wing, conventional-tail C-130 Hercules, it is much slimmer and combines *four engines with nacelles that do not show behind the wing with a symmetrical taper on both edges of the wing from the fuselage to the wing tip.*

A popular short-haul airliner, this Canadian import can carry 50 passengers from rural airports with very short runways. A few windowless models are used for air-freight operations, mostly in the Canadian back country. The Canadian Coast Guard flies a marine reconnaissance type (the DHC-7R Ranger) with bubble observer windows on the lower part of the fuselage and a belly-bulge radar dome.

Lockheed Constellation (C-69)

L1049 Super Constellation specifications: *Length:* 116'2" (35.41 m)   *Wingspan:* 123' (37.5 m)   *Cruising speed:* 260 mph (418 km/h)

A very large *four-engine, low-wing* airliner/air-cargo hauler with *triple tail fins; tail plane extends through outboard fins.*

Once the queen of the transoceanic airways, a few Connies rest on runway aprons between charter flights. Most common was the L1049, carrying up to 110 passengers, built from 1943 to 1958. A few were converted to radar planes, designated EC-121, USAF, and Navy. These had top and bottom radar bulges at the wing area of the fuselage. The rarest is the last model, the L1649, with a wing design similar to the Electra/Orion's, a straight leading edge perpendicular to the centerline of the fuselage.

Vickers Viscount 700

Length: 81'2" (24.75 m)   *Wingspan:* 94' (28.66 m)   *Cruising speed:* 315 mph (507 km/h)

A large, four-turboprop airliner with *rather large oval passenger windows; bumpy cockpit* with an odd, shouldered effect (see the de Havilland Heron, page 138, for a similar treatment); *very long, slim engine nacelles; three-piece cockpit side windows; slight dihedral in wing; sharp dihedral in tail plane.*

First prototype flown in 1948; first production 700 in 1952, carrying 40 to 59 passengers, depending on seating chosen. There is an even rarer type 800, with a stretched fuselage and 13 passenger windows, which carries up to 71 passengers. Originally named the Viceroy, after the title of the British ruler of India; renamed the Viscount after Indian independence. The world's first turboprop airliner, the Viscount managed to penetrate the American market briefly in the late 1950s.

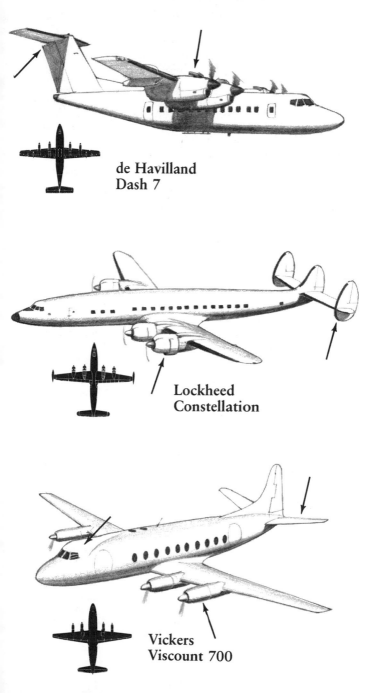

FOUR-ENGINE PROP

de Havilland
Dash 7

Lockheed
Constellation

Vickers
Viscount 700

de Havilland Heron

Length: 48'6" (14.8 m)   *Wingspan:* 71'6" (21.8 m)   *Cruising speed:* 285 mph (459 km/h) Mach 0.431

Except for the *bulging bump over the cockpit,* a wonderfully symmetrical plane. *Slight dihedral in wings and tail planes;* overhead, *symmetrically tapering wing and tail surfaces.*

Popular airframes are hard to kill: The twin-engine British transport Dove was scaled up and given four engines to become the Heron. Several private companies have put turboprop engines on Herons, the most common a Riley Turbo Skyliner. Except as executive planes, you are most likely to encounter the few remaining Herons in the Caribbean, flown by Puerto Rico International. Note the classic British touch: Engines are centered vertically on the wing.

Douglas DC4, DC6, and DC7

(Old military designations: The DC4 was the C-54 Skymaster; the DC6 was the C-118 Liftmaster)
Lengths: (DC4, DC6) 93'11" (28.6 m); (DC6A and DC6B) 100'7" (30.66 m); (DC7) 112'3" (34.21 m)   *Wingspans:* (DC4, DC6, and DC7B) 117'6" (35.8 m); DC7C 127'6" (38.86 m)   *Cruising speeds:* (DC4) 227 mph (365 km/h); (DC6) 313 (504 km/h); (DC-7) 310 mph (499 km/h)

Once you've positively identified one of the DC series, picking the specific one is a matter of size: *The only conventional-tail planes with four radial engines* in *nacelles that do not extend behind the wing's trailing edge.* (Constellation, previous page, has similar engine nacelles.) *DC4s have round windows; others are square.*

Now scarce as hen's teeth, the DC series, beginning with the pre–WWII DC4, once dominated American aviation. All powered with radial piston engines, they became increasingly uneconomical in the face of new and sophisticated turboprop aircraft and did not survive well into the jet age. As military C-54 Skymasters, they ferried troops through the Korean War era. For the few remaining, separate them from other four-engine propeller jobs by the clearly radial piston engines. (Electras and CL-44s are turboprops, with slim, forward-extending engine housings; Herons have in-line piston engines that resemble four Spitfire or Mustang noses mounted on the wings, or they have been converted to turboprops.) The unstretched DC6 has no passenger windows forward of the wing; the DC6A and DC6B have two windows ahead of the wing; DC7s have three forward windows. The last and largest of the series, the DC7C, has the wingspan increased by 5 feet on each side by the insertion of a rectangular 5-foot wing root at the fuselage, a good mark when the craft is directly overhead. In general, overhead, the DC4, DC6, and DC7 series is marked by the engines showing only forward of the leading edge and by the symmetrically tapering tail planes—the DC4 tail plane is rounded, much like an old Piper Cub's. (An Electra's leading wing edges make a straight line at right angles to the fuselage, and the tail plane edges are not symmetrical. Similar four-engine prop jobs show some nacelle behind the wing.)

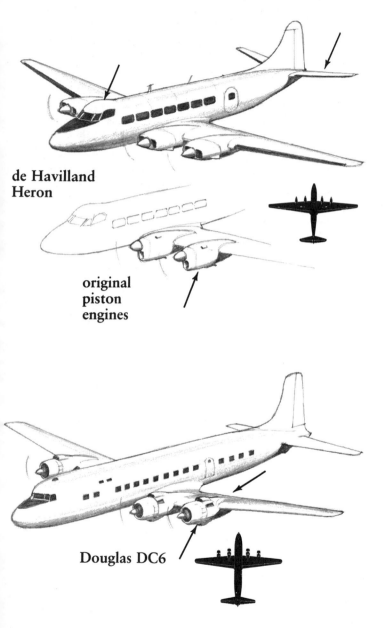

de Havilland
Heron

original
piston
engines

Douglas DC6

Lockheed L188 Electra

Length: 104'6" (31.8 m)   *Wingspan:* 99' (30.18 m)   *Cruising speed:* 405 mph (652 km/h)

Rare. Large, *low wing,* with *four turboprops; leading edge of wing straight and at right angles to fuselage; conventional tail.* Military reconnaissance version, P-3 Orion in limited use.

The jet-prop Electra came into service in 1959, just before the jet age, and in its first 18 months, its image was tarnished by two fatal crashes due to structural problems in the wing. Buyer resistance lasted until the small, true jet airliners had grabbed the commercial market. But the refitted Electras remain in service today as feeder airliners and especially as cargo planes. Like the newer CL44 and Dash 7, the turboprop Electra is much more fuel-efficient than jet aircraft, and it operates at nearly 80 percent of jet speeds. There is one possible confusion: Directly overhead, the plane resembles Lockheed's military C-130 Hercules, since you may not see that the C-130 has a high wing and an upswept rear fuselage. Note the difference in the nose shapes of the C-130 and the L188.

Canadair CL44

Length: 151'10" (46.28 m)   *Wingspan:* 142'3" (43.37 m)
Cruising speed: 380 mph (611 km/h)

Four turboprops on midwings and *ring around the tail* where the fuselage swings open; *fuselage hinged on port side; cockpit windows extend to top of fuselage:* Compare with low-wing, radial-engine DC4 series; overhead, *slim turboprop engine nacelles extend far forward of the wing's leading edge.*

The CL44 is a fuel-efficient, long-range cargo plane, with a very few passenger versions in service in Canada. Except for the massive tail fin, it looks very conventional. First flown in 1959. The hinge area forward of the tail is usually painted a color different from the rest of the fuselage. Developed from the British Britannia, as the CC-106 transport for the Canadian armed forces; then, with the swing tail, developed into the civilian CL44. CL44s are not uncommon at East Coast airports, where they haul freight on the North Atlantic routes.

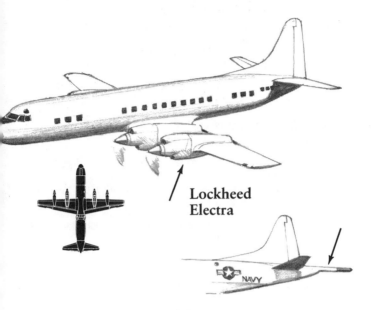

Lockheed Electra

P-3 Orion

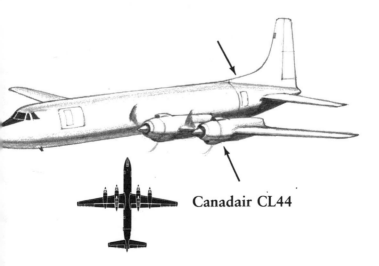

Canadair CL44

Gulfstream Aerospace Peregrine

Length: 42'1½" (12.84 m)   *Wingspan:* 39'2" (11.94 m)   *Cruising speed:* estimated 337 mph (542 km/h)

Single fanjet engine, mounted forward of the tail, slightly swept wings, small downturned winglets.

A prototype (with a *rectangular* engine intake and seven, not five, cabin windows) flew in 1983. Design derives from a prototype military trainer, reflected in the slim fuselage with only 4 feet 2 inches (1.27 m) headroom. Seats six, with crew of two. Range is subcontinental, estimated at 1600 miles (2574 km).

Israel Aircraft Industries 1123 Westwind, Commodore, Jet Commander

Length: 52'3" (15.93 m)   *Wingspan:* 44'9" (13.65 m)   *Cruising speed:* 420 mph (676 km/h)

Fuselage-mounted twin jets; conventional tail; wing tip-tanks. (The only other planes with *factory tip-tanks* and twin fuselage-mounted jets are the Learjets, which have T-tails.) High overhead, you can separate these from Learjets by the gap betweeen the wing trailing edge and the engine nacelle (the forward half of the Learjet engines rides up over the wings). The newest model, the Westwind II, has winglets on the tip-tanks.

A ten-passenger jet designed in 1963. The design was sold to Israel Aircraft after the merger of Rockwell and North American in 1967. Part of the merger agreement required the combined firms to manufacture only one executive jet, and it kept the North American Sabreliner (page 146).

Cessna Citation I, II

Citation I specifications: *Length:* 43'6" (13.26 m)   *Wingspan:* 47'1" (14.35 m)   *Cruising speed:* 420 mph (675 km/h)

The most conventional looking of all the *twin fuselage-mounted jet* executive aircraft; *unswept conventional tail plane; unswept wings tapering symmetrically.* Citation I shows distinct ventral fin.

An early entry into the exec-jet market as the Fanjet 500 in 1969. The Citation I has a wider wingspan than the Fanjet 500, whereas the Citation II's wingspan and fuselage are 5 feet longer; otherwise, they are identical. Six windows instead of four. Several hundred sold. Marketed as fuel-efficient compared to turboprops, with higher, above-the-weather ceiling.

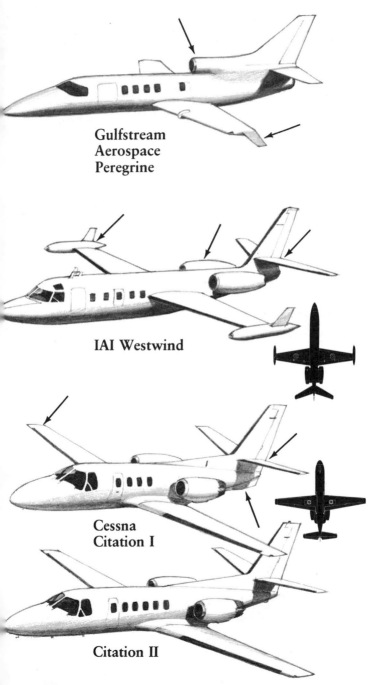

BUSINESS JETS

Gulfstream
Aerospace
Peregrine

IAI Westwind

Cessna
Citation I

Citation II

Learjet 23, 24D

Model 24D specifications: *Length:* 43'3" (12.5 m)   *Wingspan:* 35'7" (10.84 m)   *Cruising speed:* 481 mph (774 km/h)

The original small Learjet. *Fuselage-mounted twin jets reach over the wing's trailing edge; tip-tanks; wings with straight trailing edge; evenly tapered swept leading edge.*

The four-passenger Learjet 23 and the six-passenger Learjet 24 are usually distinguished by the number of windows and the tail configuration. The 23 will show two passenger windows on the right side and one on the left behind the passenger door. Most 24s show three passenger windows on the right, two on the left. Model 23s have a bullet at the center of the tail plane; most 24s do not.

Gates Learjet 25

Length: 47'7" (14.50 m)   *Wingspan:* 35'7" (10.85 m)   *Cruising speed:* 528 mph (850 km/h)

One of a family of similar Learjets. The 25 series has *five windows on the right and four on the left behind the passenger door; wings have straight trailing edge; leading edge sweeps evenly* (compare the Learjet 35 or 36); *T-tail.*

The eight-passenger 25 is the stretched version of the successful Learjet series 23/24. In a quick glance, it could be confused with the larger Learjet 35 or 36, but note the 2-foot-long equal-chord wing extension and the much larger engines on the 35 and 36.

Learjet 35, 36

Length: 48'8" (14.8 m)   *Wingspan:* 39'6" (12 m)   *Cruising speed:* 529 mph (851 km/h)

Like the Learjet 25, but with *large turbofan engines that extend above the top of the fuselage;* wings lengthened by a 2-foot equal-chord extension at the wing tip; *five windows on the right, four on the left.*

Introduced in 1973. Increased wingspan and larger engines make the 35 (eight-passenger) and 36 (luxury seating for four) capable of nonstop transcontinental or intercontinental range.

Learjet Longhorn 50 Series

Length: 55'1" (16.79 m)   *Wingspan:* 43'9" (13.34 m)   *Cruising speed:* 523 mph (842 km/h)

Fuselage bulky forward, slim aft; characteristic *upturned winglets* at wing tips; six rectangular windows right side, four on left behind passenger door; compare with the much larger Gulfstream III (page 150). Gulfstream has five oval windows on each side and a more symmetrical fuselage. Note the Longhorn's sweeping two-piece windshield compared to the numerous smaller sections in the Gulfstream III.

With seating for six to eight and 5 feet 8 inches of headroom, the new Longhorn (first delivered in 1981) was Lear's entry into the medium-sized executive jet market.

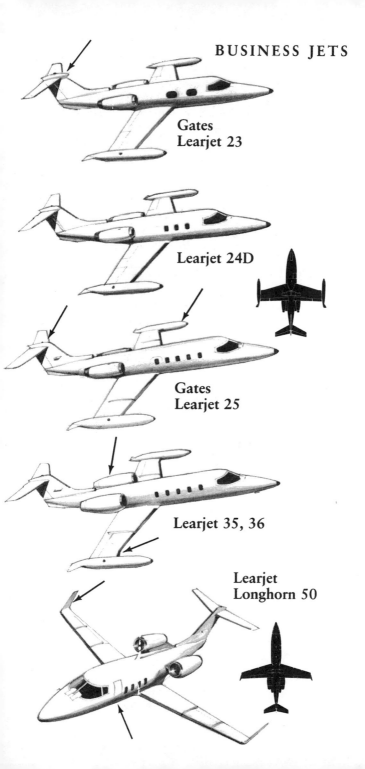

BUSINESS JETS

Gates
Learjet 23

Learjet 24D

Gates
Learjet 25

Learjet 35, 36

Learjet
Longhorn 50

North American Rockwell Sabreliner

Model 75 specifications: *Length:* 47'2" (14.38 m) *Wingspan:* 44'8" (13.61 m) *Cruising speed:* 600 mph (965 km/h)

A series of very similar aircraft with slight dimensional changes. *Twin fuselage-mounted jets; conventional tail; fully swept wings* (the Cessna Citation I and II have straight wings and conventional tail; the Falcon has swept wings with tail planes mounted midway up the fin); *very chubby* compared to similarly sized exec-jets, giving 6 feet of headroom inside.

Developed in 1958 as a utility and jet trainer for the military (supplied as T-39 and CT-39 to the USAF and the Navy), the military Sabreliners and the old model 40 had three triangular windows behind the passenger door. Later stretched versions have five triangular or square windows. The general appearance of the plane remained unchanged by modifications. Accommodates 8 to 12 passengers, depending on seating density.

Dassault Falcon 10, 100, 20, 200, HU-25, CC-117

Model 20 specifications: *Length:* 56'3" (17.15 m) *Wingspan:* 53'6" (16.29 m) *Cruising speed:* 536 mph (862 km/h)

One of two fuselage-mounted twin jets with the *tail plane midway up the tail fin* (compare the HS125/700, page 148). *Falcon tail fin has a very short fairing; strongly swept wings and tail plane.*

Popular as an executive, airline, and air-cargo plane, the Falcon 20 is being used by the U.S. Coast Guard (HU-25) and Canadian armed forces (CC-117) as a long-range patrol plane. Various passenger and cockpit window configurations, including the solid-bodied cargo craft seen at so many U.S. airports. Model 10s and 100s are 11 feet shorter in wingspan and length, with either three windows (model 10) or three port and four starboard (model 100). The Falcon 200 is a modified 20, and was introduced in 1984.

Dassault Falcon 50

Length: 60' (18.29 m) *Wingspan:* 61'10" (18.86 m) *Cruising speed:* 520 mph (837 km/h)

The only business-sized jet with *three engines, one mounted through tail fin. A miniature L1011; tail plane mounted midway up tail fin.*

Certified in 1979, the Falcon 50 is an intercontinental business and executive jet that takes the Falcon 20 airframe, adds a redesigned wing, and substitutes three smaller turbofans for the two large ones powering the 20. Used by the French govenment for VIP transportation. More than 100 sold to U.S. businesses. Carries eight passengers in extreme comfort, with a range of more than 4000 miles (6500 km).

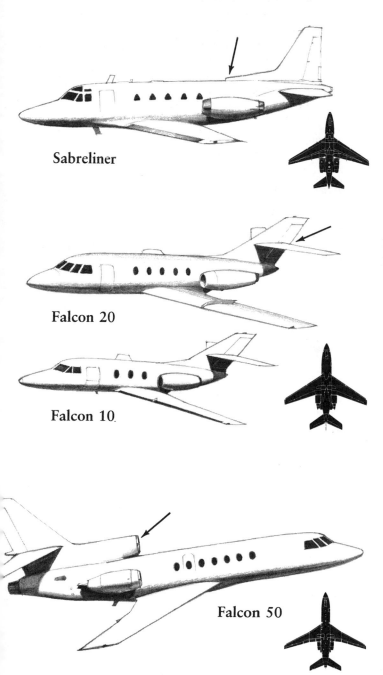

Sabreliner

Falcon 20

Falcon 10

Falcon 50

Lockheed Jetstar, C-140

Length: 60'5" (18.42 m)   *Wingspan:* 54'5" (16.60 m)   *Cruising speed:* 508 mph (817 km/h)

Uncommon, unmistakable. Combines *four rear-mounted engines* (only the huge VC10 and IL62, page 154, also have four rear engines) with *massive fuel tanks "glove mounted" on wings.*

Lockheed's partly civil, partly military light transport was produced in small numbers, including 16 Jetstar I's for the U.S. Air Force (they have slightly smaller engines than illustrated). Fewer than 100 in North America. North American's Sabreliner (page 146) got most of the military business, and Lockheed stopped building Jetstars in 1981, after 21 years of production. Crew of two; ten passengers. Complete airliner appointments, including automatic oxygen mask delivery in case of loss of pressure.

British Aerospace HS125

Length: 700, 50'8" (15.46 m)   *Wingspan:* 47' (14.33 m)   *Cruising speed:* 449 mph (722 km/h)

One of two aircraft with fuselage-mounted twin engines and *midway tail plane* (not T-tail); compare Dassault Falcon 20 (page 146). The HS125 has *moderately swept wings* (the Falcon has a strong 30-degree sweep), and the 125 shows a *noticeable tail fin fairing rising out of the fuselage over the engines and a ventral fin below the tail* (the Falcon does not). The current model 700 has six windows, right side; the older model 125 has five.

A popular business jet; more than 600 of the 125 series sold from 1965 to 1980. Stretched and streamlined model 700 carries as many as 14 passengers. When marketed in the U.S. by Beech, it was known as the Beech Hawker. The refined model 800 was introduced in 1984.

Mitsubishi Diamond

Length: 48'4" (14.7 m)   *Wingspan:* 43'5" (13.22 m)   *Cruising speed:* 343 mph (552 km/h)

One of two swept-wing, T-tailed, twin fuselage-mounted jets, without tip-tanks; compare the bulkier Canadair Challenger (page 150). The Diamond has *six oval windows that begin just behind the cockpit, including one in the passenger door.* (The Canadair Challenger has six rectangular windows that begin behind the passenger door on the right side of the aircraft.)

Japan's first entry into the business-jet market, the seven- to nine-passenger Diamond was first delivered in 1982. Like many modern aircraft, it indicates by its similarity to the Canadair the limits on the imagination imposed by the science of aeronautics. A subtle difference is the Diamond's shallow fairing from the fuselage to the tail fin; the Challenger's fin rises abruptly from the fuselage.

BUSINESS JETS

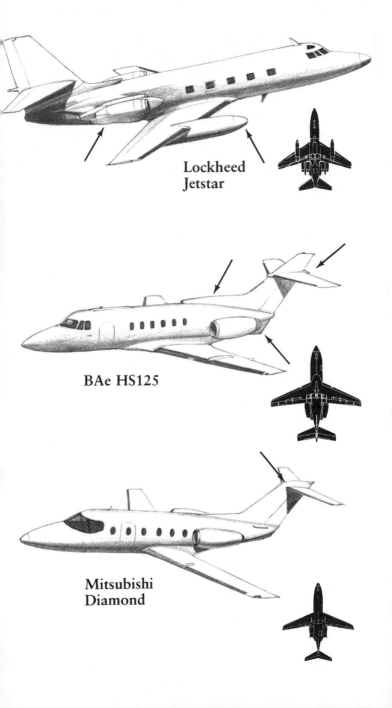

Lockheed
Jetstar

BAe HS125

Mitsubishi
Diamond

Cessna Citation III

Length: 55'5" (16.9 m)   *Wingspan: 53'4"* (16.24 m)   *Cruising speed:* 540 mph (869 km/h)

Still rare. A large plane with *twin fuselage-mounted jets and a T-tail.* Separate from similar designs by the peculiar sculpted look from the nose, flowing past the cockpit into the wing roots. *Three flap guides; "bullet" where tail planes meet fin.*

A six-passenger luxury business jet with certification to more than 51,000 feet. Capable of using relatively small airports. Initial orders in 1982 were for more than 150, indicating the interest in luxury combined with fuel efficiency—it's less fuel-efficient than buying a ticket, but that's the nature of corporate executive decision making.

Gulfstream American, Gulfstream III, IV (Grumman Gulfstream II)

Gulfstream III specifications: *Length:* 83'1" (25.32 m)   *Wingspan:* 77'10" (23.72 m)   *Cruising speed:* 512 mph (824 km/h)

A *huge business jet* (two-thirds the size of an unstretched DC9); *shallow oval windows; T-tail, fuselage-mounted twin jets.* Accommodates eight passengers and a crew of three. Intercontinental range. Model II did not have winglets. The 1983 introduction, model IV, is 2 feet longer and shows six, rather than five, passenger windows.

Grumman designed and built 258 Gulfstream IIs between 1967 and 1969. Sold to Gulfstream American (a division of American Jet Industries) and produced as the model III, with winglets, since 1980; the model IV added in 1984. The U.S. Coast Guard operates one Gulfstream II as a VIP transport, clearly marked with the CG's red diagonal stripe. Don't confuse it with the Coast Guard Falcon 20 search planes, which have the tail plane mounted halfway up the fin and round windows.

Canadair CL600 Challenger

Length: 68'6" (20.88 m)   *Wingspan:* 61'10" (18.85 m)   *Cruising speed:* 617 mph (993 km/h)

Similar to the much smaller Mitsubishi Diamond and the slightly smaller Cessna Citation III (above). *Large turbofan jets mounted on the fuselage;* strongly *swept wings; T-tail; six square windows behind passenger door;* seen overhead, *five noticeable flap guides on each wing are unique;* since 1983, with winglets. Compare the Challenger's conventional-looking nose/fuselage/wing design with the flowing sculpture of the Citation III.

Designed by the Learjet corporation and manufactured by Canadair since 1976, the Challenger is sold for business, airline, and air-cargo uses. Seats up to 30 passengers; a 5000-mile range makes it intercontinental. Passengers up to 6 feet 1 inch can stand upright in the plane, which is unusual in business craft.

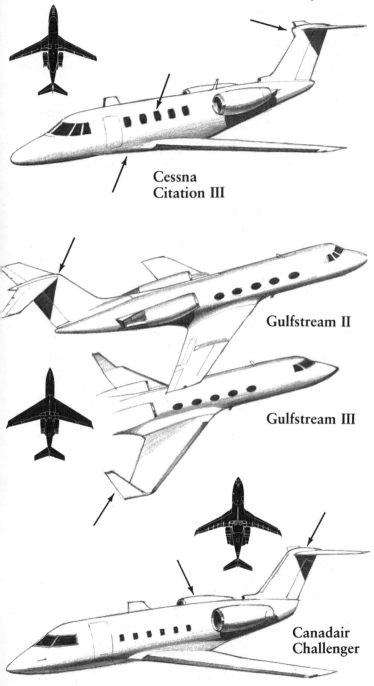

BUSINESS JETS

Cessna
Citation III

Gulfstream II

Gulfstream III

Canadair
Challenger

Aerospatiale Caravelle

Length: 105' (32.01 m)   *Wingspan:* 112'6" (34.30 m)   *Cruising speed:* 488 mph (785 km/h)

Quite rare. *Fuselage-mounted twin jets,* but easily separated from similar designs by *the tail plane mounted midway up the tail fin.* Most models also show an unusual fairing on top of the fuselage, which begins over the wings and extends into the tail plane. All models have *triangular windows.* Very clean wings without leading edge spoilers or underwing flap guides.

A masterpiece of French ingenuity first flown in 1955, it was the first airliner in the world with rear-mounted engines; what's more, the midtail compromise to get the tail planes up out of the engine turbulence was actually more successful than on the BAC111 or DC9 T-tail prototypes. There are 12 Caravelles flying that do not have the fuselage-to-tail fairing, and the plane was manufactured in several barely distinguishable lengths.

BAC 111 (One-Eleven)

Series 500 specifications: *Length:* 107' (32.61 m)   *Wingspan:* 93'6" (28.5 m)   *Cruising speed:* 461 mph (742 km/h)

A *low-wing, T-tail, fuselage-mounted twin-jet* airliner. Note four field marks separating it from the similar DC9 and Fokker Fellowship: combines *pointed nose, oval windows, three flap guides on each wing that trail behind, distinct bullet on tail plane.*

Certified in 1965 as a 79-passenger series 200 aircraft, the most common variant in the U.S. is the stretched series 500, carrying up to 119 passengers. Basically a short-haul aircraft, it is also produced in a variant for small, high-altitude, hot-weather airports: the series 475—14 feet shorter, but with the long wings and high power of the stretched 500. Now manufactured under license in Romania.

Fokker F28 Fellowship

Model Mk4000 specifications: *Length:* 97'1" (29.61 m)
Wingspan: 82'3" (25.07 m)   *Cruising speed:* 421 mph (677 km/h)

Quite rare in the U.S. *A stubby, low-wing, T-tail, fuselage-mounted, twin-jet airliner.* Separate from the much more common DC9 or BAC111 by these marks: *short, rounded nose; oval windows; distinct fairing from fuselage to tail fin; two flap guides on each wing that trail behind; squared-off rear fuselage housing a clamshell airbrake.*

Fokker attempted to cut out a particular market segment with this short-haul, high-performance aircraft. Carrying a maximum of 85 passengers in the Mk4000 configuration, the Fellowship is highly fuel-efficient and suitable for intercity hops of as little as 30 minutes' flying time. However, it has not competed successfully in the U.S. or Canada with the similarly sized DC9 series 10 and 30.

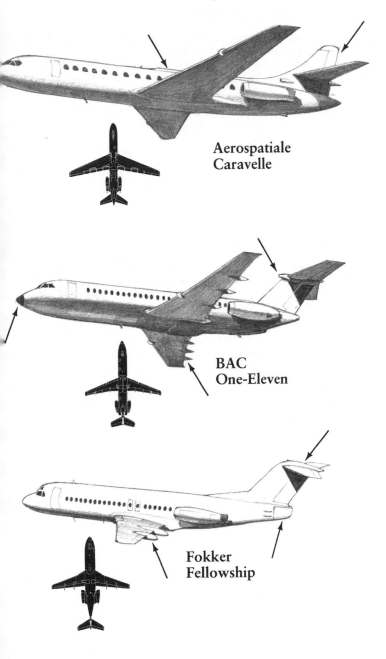

JET AIRLINERS

Aerospatiale
Caravelle

BAC
One-Eleven

Fokker
Fellowship

McDonnell Douglas DC9, MD80

Super 80 specifications: *Length:* 147'10" (45.06 m)   *Wingspan:* 107'10" (32.87 m)   *Cruising speed:* 565 mph (909 km/h)

A variety of stretched aircraft with certain common features like *fuselage-mounted twin jets and T-tail.* Field marks that distinguish DC9s from the BAC111 or Fokker Fellowship include: *rectangular windows; underwing flap guides that do not trail behind wing; no bullet on tail plane; rear fuselage tapers to a bullet behind tail fin.*
First flown in 1965 as an 80-passenger short-haul jet. Mc-Donnell Douglas always intended to stretch the plane, though not so far as the current model, the Super 80, which carries 155 passengers. Late 1960 model DC9s carrying just over 100 passengers were among the noisiest in the history of aviation, with a peculiar high-pitched whine, inside and outside the aircraft. The Super 80, renamed MD80 in 1983, is one of the quietest ever built. The smaller series, 10, 30, 40 and 50, remain DC9s.

British Aerospace VC10

Length: 158'8" (48.36 m)   *Wingspan:* 146'2" (44.55 m)   *Cruising speed:* 550 mph (885 km/h)

Quite rare. *Four fuselage-mounted jet engines; strongly swept wing and tail plane.* The only possible confusion is with the Russian Il62, an even more infrequent visitor to North America. The VC10 has a curving tail plane; the Il62 is all straight lines.
First flown in 1962, only 54 VC10s were built in all configurations, including military planes. BOAC was the only major overseas airline to purchase VC10s, and a few are still operated by Third World carriers. The plane is, and was, reliable; it gave excellent service in the high-altitude, hot-weather conditions of Africa and the Mideast. However, by the time the VC10 was certified, the intercontinental versions of the Boeing 707 (707–320) and Douglas DC8 (series 30, 40) were being sold by the hundreds. RAF tankers and transports may be seen in the U.S. and Canada.

Ilyushin Il62

Length: 174'3" (53.12 m)   *Wingspan:* 141'9" (43.20 m)   *Cruising speed:* 550 mph (885 km/h)

Very rare visitor, usually to Montréal (from Cuba and Russia) and to New York (from Russia). *Four rear-mounted jets; huge bullet at intersection of T-tail; drooped extension of outboard half of wing leading edge creates a visible break in the line.*
This is a Russian version of the Vickers VC10. Well over 100 are operating worldwide in Russia and dependent eastern-bloc countries. Maximum capacity is 186 persons, although there is at least one VIP model carrying 45 in first class and 40 more in sleeper-chair deluxe class. Outside the Russian sphere, only Egyptair ever flew them, and those were returned after the era of Russian-Egyptian goodwill ended. Look for wherever Russian delegations are traveling.

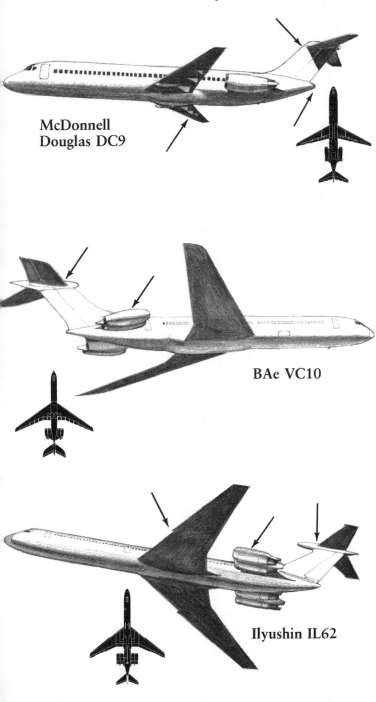

JET AIRLINERS

McDonnell
Douglas DC9

BAe VC10

Ilyushin IL62

Boeing 727

Length: 153'2" (46.69 m) *Wingspan:* 108' (32.92 m) *Cruising speed:* 570 mph (917 km/h)

The only airliner you'll see in North America with *three rear-mounted engines: one in the tail, the others on fuselage pods.* If someone should import a British Trident, it will have a distinct bullet at the center of the tail plane. The Russian military TU154 should not appear at all, but if seen elsewhere, note that it has a long pointed bullet at the tail plane.

First flown in 1963, the 727-100 (length, 133'2", 40.58 m) sold moderately to U.S. customers for medium-range flights. Since the introduction of the 727-200, which is 20 feet longer than the 727-100, Boeing has sold nearly 2000. As many as 189 passengers can fit, without much comfort, into a one-class 727-200, 90 more than the original 727-100.

McDonnell Douglas DC10, MD10

Length: 182'1" (55.50 m) *Wingspan:* 165'4" (50.41 m)
Cruising speed: 540 mph (869 km/h)

Very common at all large commercial airports, domestic and international; *wide-body jet with two wing-mounted and one rear-mounted engine; the rear engine extends straight through the tail fin.*

First carried passengers in 1971, a year before its competitor, the L1011. A variety of DC10s were built, almost all having the same external dimensions. Varying maximum ranges, payloads, or higher fuel economies are produced by varying the engines (more than six types used to date) rather than by modifying the fuselage or wings. All carry 250 passengers with a first-class section or 380 in an all-economy configuration. Renamed MD10 in 1984.

Lockheed L1011 TriStar

Length: 177'8" (54.17 m); Model 500, 165'8" (50.5 m)
Wingspan: 155'4" (47.35 m) *Cruising speed:* 558 mph (898 km/h)

A *jumbo wide-body; two engines on wings; one rear-mounted at tail.* Separate from the DC10 by noting that the *tail-mounted engine has intake above the fuselage and exhausts through end of the fuselage.* Compare the DC10 tail engine, which carries straight through the tail fin.

A popular wide-body that has never suffered from a single serious mechanical defect, the L1011 was sold for only ten years, 1972–1982, before Lockheed withdrew from the passenger jet field, leaving it to Boeing and McDonnell Douglas, whose DC10 was a direct competitor to the L1011. Fewer than 300 are in service. The long-range model 500 is not noticeably shorter, but it can be picked out on the flight line by the way the tail engine is faired directly into the fuselage (see sketch above model drawing).

JET AIRLINERS

Boeing 727

McDonnell
Douglas DC10

Lockheed L1011

Boeing 767

Length: 159'2" (48.51 m)   *Wingspan:* 156'4" (47.65 m)   *Cruising speed:* 506 mph (814 km/h)

Fat-bodied, with *two huge turbofans* mounted under the wing. Compare the Airbus A300 (next entry). The 767 is 16 feet shorter than the Airbus, but the easiest diagnostic difference is that the *three* (not five) *flap guides barely extend behind the wing.* Two, not three, passenger doors. Dihedral in tail plane.

The competition between the Airbus, introduced in 1979, and the 1982 Boeing 767 is expected to be intense. The Boeing entry, depending on the engine and the passenger configuration, has a potentially longer range, 3545 miles (5705 km) compared to the A300's 2530 miles (4074 km), making the 767 suitable for transcontinental and shorter intercontinental routes, but 1984 saw new, long-range versions of one A300.

Airbus A300

Length: 175'11" (53.62 m)   *Wingspan:* 147'1" (44.84 m)
Cruising speed: 515 mph (829 km/h)

A *fat-bodied* airliner with *two huge turbofans mounted below and forward of the wing. Compare the Boeing 767* (previous entry). Close at hand or overhead, the Airbus is not difficult to distinguish from the Boeing 767. Note the *five flap track guides on each wing that extend well behind the trailing edge.* Also, the Airbus has *three passenger doors* and *one galley door set behind the wing.*

Built by a consortium of French, British, West German, and Spanish aircraft companies, the A300 carries up to 390 passengers. The A300s are noticeable, as are the Boeing 767s, in airport traffic patterns because they climb much more slowly than other jet airliners. Their similarity indicates how few options are actually available to aircraft engineers seeking a short- to medium-range wide-body.

Boeing 737 (200 and 300)

737-200 specifications: *Length:* 100' (30.48 m)   *Wingspan:* 93' (28.35 m)   *Cruising speed:* 564 mph (907 km/h)

A *stubby twin jet* that gives the illusion, by its shortness, of being a wide-body. The 737-200 is unique, the only twin-engine on which the *nacelles extend in front of and behind the wing.* The 737-300, with twin fan jets, resembles the A300 or Boeing 767 but is only half as big. Overhead, where size is difficult to judge, the 737-300 shows *one large and two small flap guides extending behind the wing.* Compare the A300, which shows five flap guides, and the 767, on which four guides are barely visible.

The primary short-haul jet of the 1970s, the 737-200, with only 130 passengers and a short takeoff and landing ability, could operate from regional airports and even be modified to use gravel airstrips. The 737-300 is 9 feet 7 inches (2.9 m) longer and carries 140 passengers.

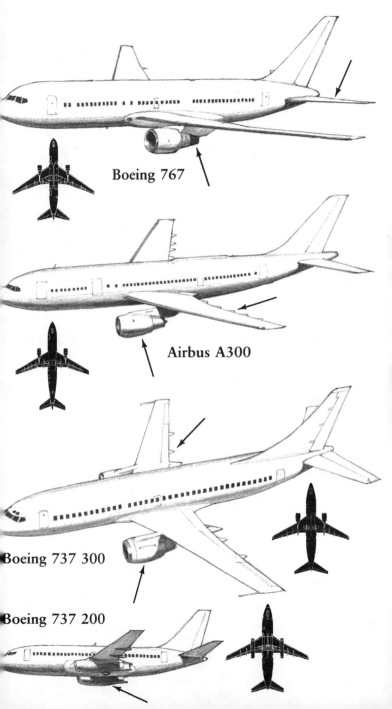

JET AIRLINERS

Boeing 767

Airbus A300

Boeing 737 300

Boeing 737 200

Boeing 757

Length: 154'8" (47.14 m)   *Wingspan:* 124'6" (37.95 m)   *Cruising speed:* 494 mph (795 km/h)

Slim-bodied, with *two large turbofans* mounted under the wing, *showing well forward* of the wing. This plane should separate easily from the wide-bodied, twin-turbofan airplanes, but compare it to the Airbus A-300 and the Boeing 737 and 767. The combination of normal fuselage and engines is diagnostic.

From the passenger's point of view, the 757 is nothing more than a stretched, re-engined version of Boeing's popular 727 aircraft. Other differences are subtle, but include a wing with less sweepback and greater depth (chord). The 757 is 19 feet longer than the 727. Like the stretched DC9, the 757 carries more passengers and is certified to fly with two, rather than three, flight officers—a considerable saving.

McDonnell Douglas DC8

Series 60 specifications: *Length:* 187'5" (57.12 m)   *Wingspan:* 148'5" (45.23 m)   *Cruising speed:* 600 mph (965 km/h)

A series of *four-engine jet liners.* Compare with the Boeing 707-720 (next entry) before deciding. The most common variant is the extreme stretch Series 60: Viewed at any distance, it has the aspect of great fuselage length balanced on relatively negligible wings. On the ground, the tail fin has no vhf radio antenna (compare the 707 drawing); *smooth, cigar-shape engine nacelles; distinct "brow" at cockpit window; tail fin swept;* but *stretch 60 series even more radically swept.*

A popular airliner first flown in 1958. Most have been converted, whatever their original size, into the super stretches by the insertion of fuselage plugs fore and aft of the wings. Series 70 is a stretch with more efficient, quieter fan engines. Still flown by many economy overseas airlines.

Boeing 707, 720

707-320 specifications: *Length:* 152'11" (46.61 m)   *Wingspan:* 145'9" (44.42 m)   *Cruising speed:* 550 mph (885 km/h)

The 707 has a superficial resemblance to the Douglas DC8, but once you have identified the plane by some minor details, its configuration is quite different and instantly recognizable. *Four engines on wing, engine nacelles are distinctly larger forward* (compare the much smoother, cigarlike DC8 nacelles). *The engines are tucked up under the wing* (the DC8 engines carried a bit lower and a bit farther forward). *The cockpit windows are very close to the nose* (the DC8 has more nose to it).

The first U.S.-built jet liner, flown in 1954. Very successful; made in a number of variations for increased passenger capacity or for transoceanic flights. The similar 720 was a medium-range plane with thinner, slightly more swept wings and a distinct ventral fin. Alas, a few 707s (model 420) also carry the ventral fin. To muddle the issue further, American Airlines designated its 720s as 707-023s. Call them 707s until you're reading the in-flight safety card.

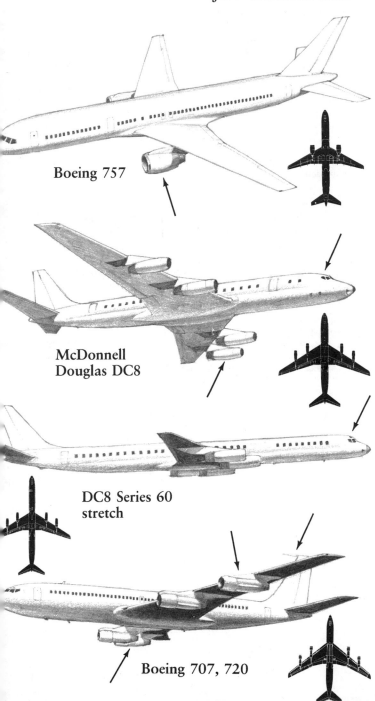

JET AIRLINERS

Boeing 757

McDonnell
Douglas DC8

DC8 Series 60
stretch

Boeing 707, 720

British Aerospace BAe146-200

Length: 93'8" (28.55 m)   *Wingspan:* 86'5" (26.34 m)   *Cruising speed:* 440 mph (708 km/h)

New in 1982. Smallest of the four-engined jets; *massive fin to T-tail* (not unlike de Havilland's Dash turboprops); *large flap tracks underwing—bulging landing gear fairings on belly;* the only four-jet-on-the-wing T-tail.

Designed over several years, beginning in 1973, by the ailing British aerospace industry, the BAe146 is a short-haul jet that takes advantage of modern fan-jet engines to produce a quiet aircraft; it can land and take off in cities without annoying airport neighbors. First American purchase by Air Wisconsin. Built with many partners to share risk of tooling up: Wings and engines by Avco (U.S.), engine cowlings by Short Brothers (Northern Ireland), tail by Saab (Sweden).

Boeing 747 (747SP and 747-300)

747 specifications: *Length:* 231'4" (70.51 m)   *Wingspan:* 195'8" (59.64 m)   *Cruising speed:* 550 mph (885 km/h)

Unmistakable. The *four-engine jumbo jet with the bulge behind the cockpit.* Some variants are rarer and more fun to identify: The earliest model 100s had a short upper cabin, showing three side windows; the super long-range 747SP (special purpose) is 47 feet shorter (bottom drawing). The newest model 300 (top sketch) has lengthened the top deck passenger area and carries 69 passengers "upstairs," compared to 32 passengers in the late 100 and 200 models.

The 747, first flown in 1969 and still the heaviest airliner in the world, began in design as Boeing's entry in a heavy-lift military contract competition. When Lockheed, and its controversial C-5A Galaxy, was chosen in 1965, Boeing concentrated on turning the heavy-lifter into the world's first wide-body passenger jet, carrying 350 to 400 persons. The plane has had a remarkable mechanical safety record, with the few accidents all involving pilot error. Look for the SP variant at international airports.

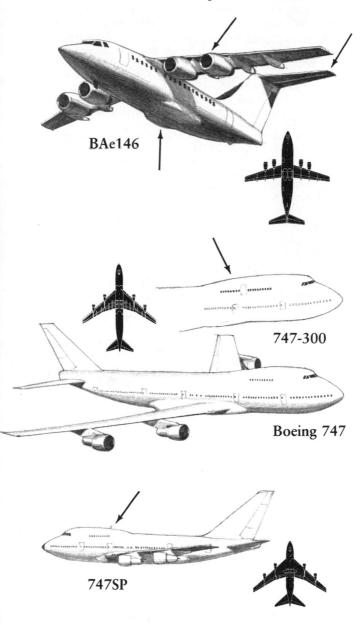

JET AIRLINERS

BAe146

747-300

Boeing 747

747SP

Convair 880, 990

990 specifications: *Length:* 139'2" (42.41 m)   *Wingspan:* 120'
(36.58 m)   *Cruising speed:* 556 mph (895 km/h)

A pair of curious airliners that are hardly ever seen, and then
usually parked at the air-cargo flight line of southern U.S. airfields.
Not unlike a DC8. The 990 is easily distinguished by two *anti-
shock fairings that trail behind each wing.*

The 880 has perfectly smooth, cigar-shaped engine nacelles and
skinny antiturbulence booms on the tips of the tail planes.

Convair's last passenger planes, the 880 and 990 were financial
disasters for the company. A total of 102 of both models were
built. A narrow fuselage with a maximum five-abreast seating and
low fuel economy doomed the project. The few North American
survivors, included here for historical interest, are in the southern
U.S. They are typically used for specialty air-cargo service, particularly flying live cattle from U.S. breeders to South American
ranches.

Aerospatiale/BAC Concorde

Length: 203'9" (62.10 m)   *Wingspan:* 83'10" (25.55 m)   *Cruising
speed:* 1336 mph (2150 km/h)

Rare, but seen frequently at Kennedy airport, Dulles, and
Miami. *Long, skinny fuselage with delta wings; four rectangular
air intakes under wing; no tail planes at all.*

First flown in 1971; first passengers, 1975. After environmental
complaints about sonic booms and upper-atmosphere air pollution,
airport noise, and the quadrupling of the price of petroleum, the
once-hopeful supersonic Concorde was dropped by every airline
(more than 70 were on order at one time), except for the govern-
ment-subsidized airlines of the manufacturing countries, British
Airways and Air France. Can carry 128 passengers across the Atlantic in less than 3 hours.

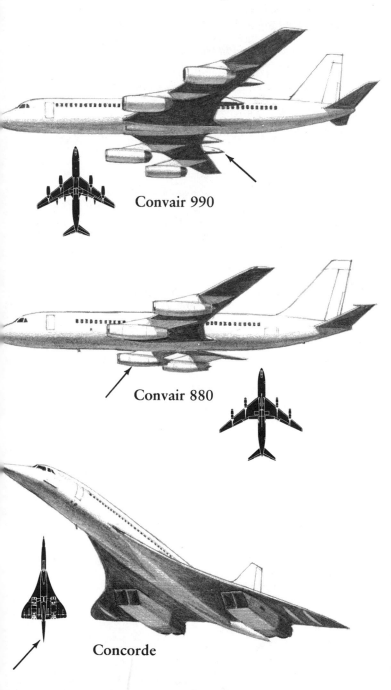

Convair 990

Convair 880

Concorde

Beech T-34C

Length: 28'8" (8.72 m)   *Wingspan:* 33'4" (10.16 m)   *Level flight:* 241 mph (388 km/h)

The Navy's only *slim-nosed, propeller-driven* airplane. *High greenhouse canopy; ventral fin; finlet fairings to tail plane; paired airscoops; large side exhausts.*

The latest in a long line of Navy-style in-line trainers, including the SN-J (Texan) and the nonturbocharged Beech T-34 it replaces (page 46). The T-34C, with turboprop, is 90 mph faster than the T-34, making it an easier step up to the 343 mph T-28 Trojan used for carrier training (page 44). As with many trainers, it can be fitted with armaments and sold overseas for counterinsurgency missions.

Rockwell OV-10 Bronco

Length: 41'7" (12.67 m)   *Wingspan:* 40' (12.19 m)   *Cruising speed:* 210 mph (338 km/h)

Overhead, the *perfectly rectangular wing and tail plane* are diagnostic; on the ground, the twin booms to the tail extend naturally out of the fuselage. The Cessna Skymaster is the only similar aircraft.

The little OV-10 is a short takeoff and landing observation and counterinsurgency aircraft that can operate without arresting gear from runways as short as the deck of a helicopter-carrying amphibious assault ship. A few heavily armed versions are in service with the U.S. Marines, including models for night observation: These have a distinctive probe extending from the nose that houses a forward-looking infrared sensor and laser used to guide missiles to the target. They are usually seen near bombing ranges, circling over practicing attack aircraft at a leisurely 55 mph.

Grumman OV-1 Mohawk

Length: 41' (12.5 m)   *Wingspan:* 48' (14.63 m)   *Level flight:* 289 mph (465 km/h)

Bulbous cockpit and *triple tail* give a sort of dragonfly look to the craft; *wing tanks* and a *right-side radar pod extend forward of nose.*

The Mohawk has such odd geometry that it can hardly be compared to any other aircraft ever flown. Though not all models have the curious radar pod that extends past the nose, the Grumman-style dihedral tail plane and triple tail fins are enough for positive identification. Most OV-1s carry two underwing fuel tanks just outboard of the engines. Only the Army flies the Mohawk, which is used as a target locater and battlefield mapper. The heavily armed Mohawks of the Vietnam War have been refitted, as the Air Force, Navy, and Marines captured the fixed-wing attack plane mission from Army aviation.

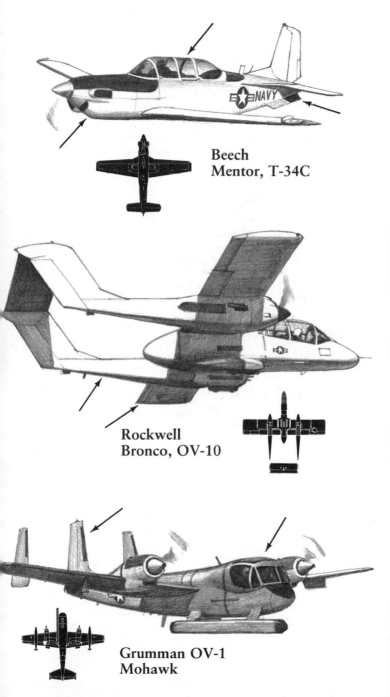

MILITARY AIRCRAFT

Beech
Mentor, T-34C

Rockwell
Bronco, OV-10

Grumman OV-1
Mohawk

Grumman E-2 Hawkeye and C-2 Greyhound

Length: 57'7" (17.6 m)   *Wingspan:* 80'7" (24.6 m)   *Cruising speed:* 296 mph (476 km/h)

The E-2 is an unmistakable *twin-engine* aircraft backpacking a *30-foot-diameter radar pancake.* The C-2 utility version is the *only high-wing twin prop with four tail fins.*

The Hawkeye's mission is early warning for the carrier fleet. The Greyhound serves as a shore-to-ship delivery system, carrying up to 39 passengers or 4 tons of freight. The type has certain Grumman characteristics, including a dihedral in the tail planes and engines that angle out slightly from the fuselage. (Note those features in Grumman's smaller OV-1, previous entry, which has three tail fins.) Overhead, it is the only twin-engine propeller aircraft that combines a straight trailing edge to the tail plane with symmetrically tapering wings.

Lockheed P-2 Neptune

Length: 91'8" (27.94 m)   *Wingspan:* 103'10" (31.65 m)   *Cruising speed:* 230 mph (370 km/h)

Extraordinarily rare. Last craft based at Roosevelt Roads, Puerto Rico. Two engines, *midwing* with characteristic Lockheed wing design: *straight leading edge at right angles to fuselage* with *tip-tanks.*

From the side or below, the old-fashioned clear Plexiglas nose compartment separates the Neptune quickly from other operational twin-engine planes. First flown in 1947, the land-based Neptune's long-range capability is given away by the typical wingspan of such aircraft: The plane is clearly wider than long, even including the rear magnetic probe. Japan, with much coastline and no aircraft carriers, has adopted the P-2 airframe, and the Kawasaki company has built dozens of them for the Naval Self-Defense Force.

Grumman S-2 Tracker, Trader and E-1 Tracer

Length: 43'6" (13.26 m)   *Wingspan:* 72'7" (22.13 m)   *Cruising speed:* 150 mph (241 km/h)

Increasingly rare. In service as the Trader only, a shore-to-ship cargo plane; *twin engines that extend fore and aft* of the *symmetrically tapering wings;* strong *dihedral in tail planes.*

A typical Grumman aircraft. Note the bug-eyed cockpit (see the Mohawk, previous page). When it was outfitted for advance warning of aircraft, it carried a teardrop-shaped radar dome 30 feet long (compare the current early-warning Hawkeye, with its round radar pod). Seen overhead, it could conceivably be confused with some commercial twin-engines, but the following combination is unique: symmetrically tapered wings; engine nacelles that extend well behind the wing; and a straight-line trailing edge on the tail plane.

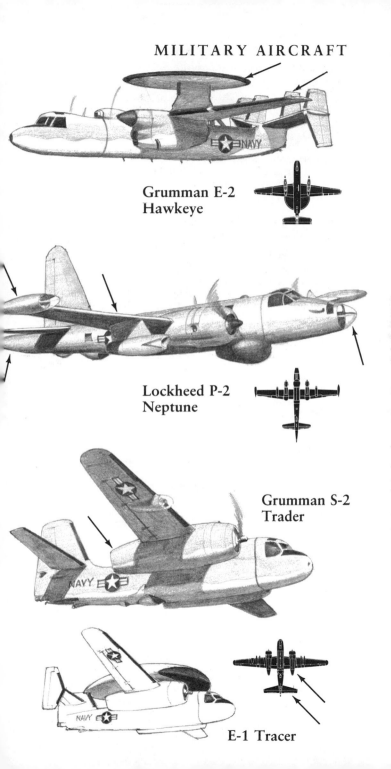

MILITARY AIRCRAFT

Grumman E-2 Hawkeye

Lockheed P-2 Neptune

Grumman S-2 Trader

E-1 Tracer

de Havilland C-8A Buffalo

Length: 79' (24.08 m)   *Wingspan:* 96' (29.26 m)   *Cruising speed:* 261 mph (420 km/h)

Fairly common military transport in the U.S. and Canada. *Combination of twin turboprop engines, upswept fuselage, and T-tail* is unique. There is a slight resemblance, at a distance, to the twin-engine Dash 8 commercial airliner.

The Buffalo is noticeably bulkier than the midtailed Caribou. The overhead view is much like the Caribou, the leading edge of the wing almost, but not quite, straight; the tail plane almost, but not quite, rectangular. In commercial service, it is designated DHC5; in Canadian armed forces, CC-115.

de Havilland C-7A Caribou

Length: 72'7" (22.13 m)   *Wingspan:* 95'7" (29.15 m)   *Cruising speed:* 182 mph (293 km/h)

Fuselage *strongly upswept, "bent up"* to tail plane with *midfin tail plane;* overhead, *straight leading edge wings, sharply tapered trailing edges from engines to wing tips.*

This durable short takeoff and landing freighter serves in the U.S. Air Force (after transfer from the Army), in the Canadian armed forces (designated CC-108), and in bush country air-freight and passenger work (as DHC4A). There are other upswept fuselage planes, but only the Caribou has the "bent" look plus the reverse gull-wing effect as the wings droop down to the engines and then angle up to the tips. First flown in 1958, it uses radial piston engines.

Fairchild C-123 Provider

Length: 76'3" (23.93 m)   *Wingspan:* 110' (33.53 m)   *Cruising speed:* 228 mph (367 km/h)

Fairly rare. *Upsweep* of fuselage *begins atop the wing; two radial engines; conventional tail plane.*

The last active military C-123s are at Westover Air Force Base, near Springfield, Massachusetts. The twin-engine C-123 bears only the slightest resemblance to other upswept-fuselage aircraft—its sheer bulk and the straight line of the upsweep into the conventional tail separate it automatically from the de Havilland Caribou (midway tail plane) and Buffalo (T-tail) (previous entries). Widely used in Vietnam, it was the principal aircraft for defoliant spraying, and it can be seen occasionally in this country performing insecticide spraying missions for the U.S. Forest Service or the Bureau of Land Management. Overhead, it is fat and noisy.

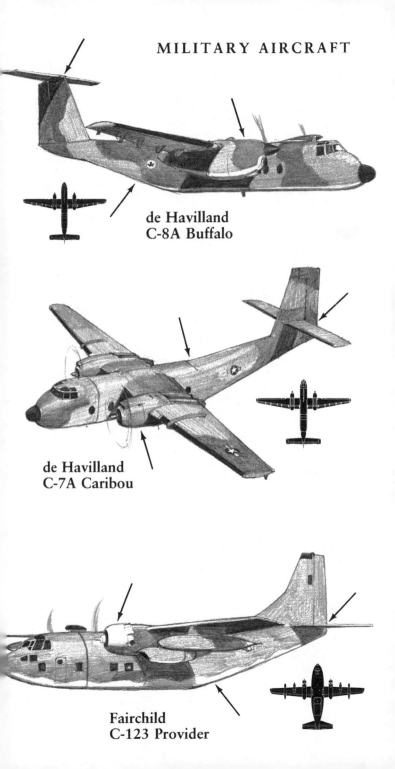

de Havilland
C-8A Buffalo

de Havilland
C-7A Caribou

Fairchild
C-123 Provider

Lockheed C-130 Hercules

Length: 97'10" (29.78 m)   *Wingspan:* 132'7" (40.41 m)   *Cruising speed:* 340 mph (547 km/h)

Common, nationwide. *Combines upswept fuselage with conventional tail, radar dome nose,* and classic Lockheed wing; *straight leading edge at right angles to fuselage;* four turboprop engines.

The bulky C-130 bears no real resemblance, even overhead, to the more elegant and T-tailed de Havilland Dash 7 (page 137). (There is a Russian copy of the Hercules, the An-12 Cub.) Compare the overhead view of the Hercules with the Electra (page 141). The Hercules is bulkier, and its radar dome nose looks comical. The Orion's is simply the curved nose of the airplane. C-130s are operated by all four U.S. services in modes from gunships to weather observation and search and rescue, as well as transports. The C-130 was the type of aircraft used by the Israeli government on the successful mission to free the hijacked Air France passengers at Entebbe, Uganda, on July 3, 1976.

Rockwell T-2 Buckeye

Length: 38'4" (11.66 m)   *Wingspan:* 38'10" (11.62 m)   *Level flight:* 522 mph (840 km/h) Mach 0.69 at sea level

Seen near naval flight schools and stateside aircraft carriers. *Large canopy* for tandem pilot and instructor; straight wings with tip-tanks; a *stubby, front-heavy look.*

The Navy's basic jet trainer used for teaching pilots to land on an aircraft carrier. It resembles the side-by-side seating USAF T-37 if the wing geometry is not visible. The T-2's engine intakes are well forward of the wing. First built as a single-engine trainer by North American, based on the Navy's retired FJ-1 Fury fighters. The twin version is all that flies today, and later models are the first Navy planes with fiber-glass wings. Rockwell also markets it as a counterinsurgency plane.

Lockheed T-33A Trainer (type of F-80 Shooting Star)

Length: 37'8" (11.48 m)   *Wingspan:* 38'9" (11.85 m)   *Level flight:* 600 mph (965 km/h) Mach 0.9 at altitude

Rare. More common in Canada, U.S. sightings unlikely except near Anchorage, Alaska, and Hickham Field, in Oahu, Hawaii. *Tapering unswept wings* with *prominent tip-tanks.* In side view, a cigar with a tandem-seating canopy.

The original USAF F-80 Shooting Star was converted to a trainer by adding 3 feet to the cockpit to accommodate two pilots in tandem. The F-80 participated in the first all-jet dogfight, when one shot down a MiG-15 at the beginning of the Korean War. More than 100 are in service with the Royal Canadian Air Force, many built in Canada under license. More than 100 are in U.S. service, used for radar training and to impersonate unfriendly aircraft in war games.

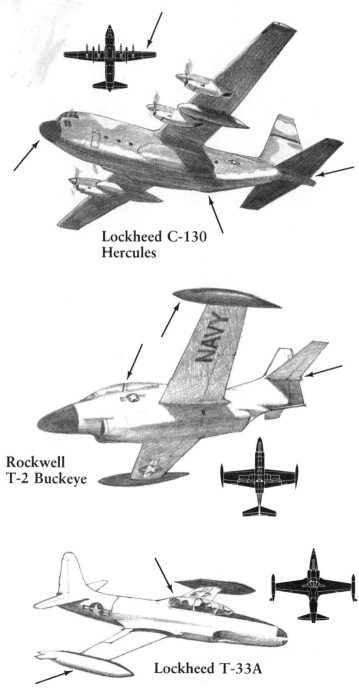

MILITARY AIRCRAFT

Lockheed C-130
Hercules

Rockwell
T-2 Buckeye

Lockheed T-33A

Cessna A-37 Dragonfly and T-37

Length: 29'4" (8.92 m)   *Wingspan:* 33'7" (10.3 m)   *Level flight:* 507 mph (816 km/h) Mach 0.658 at sea level

Low straight wings with conspicuous tip-tanks and inconspicuous twin jets at the wing roots; bulbous cockpit for side-by-side seating in the trainer version. Nothing else flying has *twin wing-root jets and straight wings at right angles to the fuselage.*

Though many combat aircraft have been converted to trainers, the counterinsurgency A-37B was developed as a gunship from the USAF's standard jet trainer, the T-37. It saw wide use in areas of Vietnam not defended by surface-to-air missiles, carrying a 7.62-mm minigun capable of firing 6000 rounds a minute as well as cluster and phosphorus bombs. Suitable for use against lightly armed "insurgents," the A-37's low stall speed, under 100 mph, makes it a precision instrument.

Canadair CL41, CT-114 Tutor

Length: 32' (9.75 m)   *Wingspan:* 36'5" (11.13 m)   *Level flight:* 488 mph (785 km/h) Mach 0.64 at sea level

Seen only in Canada in North America. *Small,* with a *very slim rear fuselage; T-tail; large canopy* covers side-by-side, two-man cockpit; *quite small air intakes forward of wing root.*

A somewhat variable Canadian trainer. First flown in 1960, adopted by the RCAF in 1964. RCAF weapons instruction models will show hard points on the lower side of the wing for carrying bombs or rockets. The extremely slim rear fuselage is almost a Canadian style. Note the old propeller trainer, the de Havilland Chipmunk (page 24).

Fairchild NGT, T-46

Length: 29'6" (9.0 m)   *Wingspan:* 37' (11.3 m)   *Level flight:* 495 mph (796 km/h) Mach 0.642 at altitude

A 1983 introduction. *Combines twin tail fins with straight wings, twin jet engines mounted at wing roots.* The only other twin-fin, straight wing jet is the A-10 Thunderbolt, but it has massive engines mounted on the rear fuselage. T-46 wings droop (negative dihedral).

Fairchild's experience with the A-10 went directly into this winning entry in the N(ext) G(eneration) T(rainer) competition for a replacement for the Cessna T-37 jet trainer. The T-46 can take off and land in two-thirds the distance of the T-37, allowing it to use civilian airports—always useful for a training plane. Part of the success in winning the contract came from building a flyable 62 percent size model out of the same composite materials used in Rutan's home-built Long-Ez aircraft (page viii).

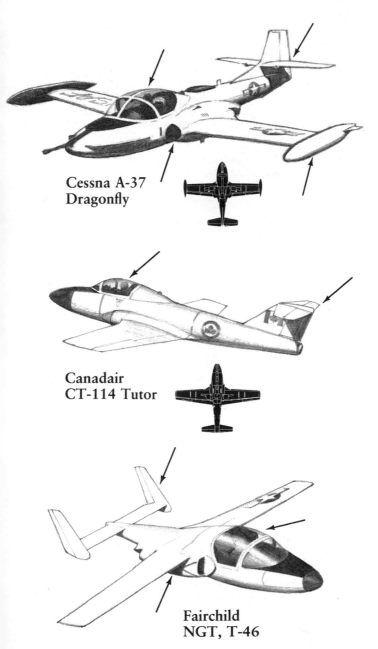

Cessna A-37
Dragonfly

Canadair
CT-114 Tutor

Fairchild
NGT, T-46

Fairchild Republic A-10 Thunderbolt

Length: 53'4" (16.25 m)   *Wingspan:* 57'6" (17.53 m)   *Level flight:* 443 mph (713 km/h) Mach 0.58 at sea level

Fuselage-mounted huge turbofan twin jets rise *above the fuselage;* overhead, note the *rectangular tail plane.*

The A-10 is a highly maneuverable ground support plane, essentially an aircraft wrapped around a 30-millimeter gun that fills the inside of the fuselage. The ammunition is typically simple cylinders of depleted (not radioactive) uranium that destroy tanks by mere impact. The A-10 is basically an alternative to smart bombs and heat-seeking missile systems, and relies heavily on the pilot, instead of sophisticated instrumentation, for success. Occasionally seen in Florida and Arizona near firing ranges, but based in Wisconsin, New York, Connecticut, Massachusetts, and Maryland. Also seen at Nomans Land, off Martha's Vineyard in Massachusetts. Some authors allege a resemblance to the Cessna Citation, though there is none.

Fairchild Republic F-105 Thunderchief

Length: 69'1" (21 m)   *Wingspan:* 35' (10.66 m)   *Level flight:* 1485 mph (2389 km/h) Mach 2.2 at altitude

Rare. National Guard and USAF Reserve only. On the ground or overhead, the *outswept air intakes* are all you need to identify it; *strongly swept wing, tail plane, and tail fin.*

The Thunderchief was a well-designed airframe looking for a mission. Though intended as a long-range nuclear bomber with fighter maneuverability, that mission was scrapped in the late 1950s in favor of B-52s and ICBMs. Converted to conventional bombs carried externally, the 105 was heavily used in Vietnam, where more than 400, half the total production, were shot down by missiles and MiGs. These heavy losses convinced the Air Force to convert the two-seat trainer version of the F-105 to a radar-suppression role, carrying a radar officer behind the pilot.

British Aerospace AV-8A Harrier

Length: 45'6" (13.9 m)   *Wingspan:* 25'3" (7.7 m)   *Level flight:* 737 mph (1186 km/h) Mach 0.95 at sea level

High *droopy wings,* on the airfield; *wing tip landing gear; massive air intakes* well forward of the wings are especially noticeable overhead.

The AV-8A Harriers in service with the U.S. Marine Corps have a bulky shouldered look, and the directable engine exhausts are under the balance point of the aircraft, giving it the unique ability to take off vertically. The Harrier gave the Marines a long-sought dream, a close-support fighter-bomber that would be positioned near the troops and clearly under Marine command, not subject to the orders of Navy carriers or Air Force base commanders. McDonnell Douglas is now building more than 300 of the more capable AV-8B version.

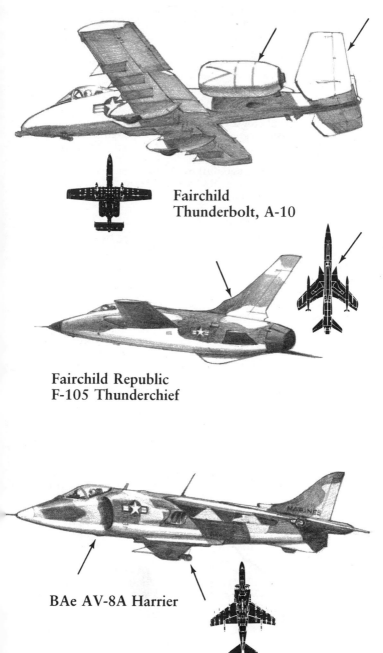

MILITARY AIRCRAFT

Fairchild
Thunderbolt, A-10

Fairchild Republic
F-105 Thunderchief

BAe AV-8A Harrier

Grumman A-6 Intruder/EA-6 Prowler

A-6 specifications: *Length:* 54'7" (16.64 m)   *Wingspan:* 53'
(16.15 m)   *Level flight:* 625 mph (1006 km/h) Mach 0.82 at sea
level

The *twin jet engines mounted at the wing roots,* combined with
swept wings, are diagnostic and give the plane its characteristic,
bulky forward, slim aft look. Up close, note the hooked-nose electronic probe in front of the cockpit.

The Navy's basic night/all-weather bomber since 1960, the A-6A
was heavily used during the Vietnam War along with the newer
Air Force F-111s for night precision bombing. The basic airplane,
with side-by-side seating, has been modified into a radar and communications jamming craft, the EA-6A. A four-seat version, the
EA-6B, has even more sophisticated antielectronics capacity. Both
EA versions are distinguished by the electronic pod on the tail fin;
what appear to be externally mounted bombs on the EA-6Bs are
additional wing-mounted electronics.

Vought F-8 Crusader

Length: 54'6" (16.6 m)   *Wingspan:* 35'2" (10.71 m)   *Level flight:*
1200 mph (1931 km/h) Mach 1.6 at sea level

Rare. A few with naval and marine reserve units; very few active
in Navy as photo-reconnaissance craft. Looks like an *aircraft built
around an engine.* Compare the A-7 Corsair, which looks like a
plane *built on top of a jet engine.* The *distinct hump over the wing*
houses machinery that alters the pitch (incidence) of the entire
wing for takeoff and landing.

From the late 1950s to the late 1960s, the standard day-fighter
of the Navy. The active naval versions are remarkably clean aircraft—no tip-tanks, no armament, no radar or electronic warfare
bulges; just barely noticeable camera lenses on the underside of the
fuselage. Reserve aircraft may be carrying underwing armament or
fuel tanks.

Vought A-7 Corsair II

Length: 46'1" (14 m)   *Wingspan:* 38'8" (11./8 m)   *Level flight:*
698 mph (1123 km/h) Mach 0.9 at sea level

Standard aboard carriers, rare on land. *Very large air intake and
exhaust;* overhead, note the *slim, strongly swept tail plane;* in any
view, the *bulky fuselage without apparent taper;* inland, you're
probably looking at an Air Force Vought F-8 (preceding entry).

The Navy's standard attack bomber, roughly based on the USAF
F-8 design, has a stubbier, bulbous nose and deeper air intakes,
giving it a much different profile. A subtle, unique field mark of the
A-7 is the vertical squaring off of the tail sail; this notching allows
a few more A-7s to be packed onto a carrier hangar deck. Viewed
from beneath, the A-7s and F-8s are almost identical, with the A-7
having the larger wing surface area. They're not likely to be distinguished unless both airplanes are in the air together. The A-7s remain operational with the regular Navy and Marines.

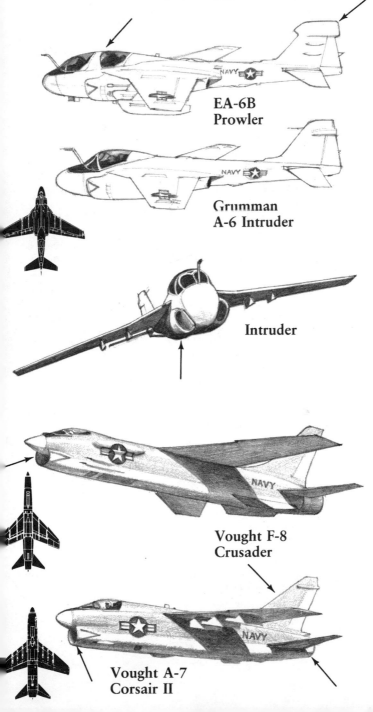

MILITARY AIRCRAFT

EA-6B
Prowler

Grumman
A-6 Intruder

Intruder

Vought F-8
Crusader

Vought A-7
Corsair II

General Dynamics (Convair) F-106 Delta Dart

Length: 70'8" (21.5 m)   *Wingspan:* 38'3" (11.66 m)   *Level flight:* 1525 mph (2454 km/h) Mach 2.28 at altitude

Rare. National Guard and USAF Reserve. *Pure delta wing; easily distinguished, when overhead, from variable-geometry craft by the engine exhaust extending well behind wing trailing edge.*

The only delta-wing craft operational in the U.S., the F-106 is based with a few Air Force Reserve units from Cape Cod to California. Designed to intercept attacking intercontinental bombers, the F-106 carries a cannon as well as air-to-air guided missiles in an interior bomb bay. Carries a pair of underwing fuel tanks. A few tandem-seat cockpit models were built. With a maximum pursuit speed of more than 1700 mph (Mach 2.3), it remains one of the fastest single-engine aircraft ever built.

McDonnell Douglas F-4 Phantom

Length: 58'–63' (17.7 m–19.2 m)   *Wingspan:* 38'4" (11.7 m)
Level flight: up to 1500 mph (2414 km/h) Mach 2.25 at altitude

Look for the *drooping tail planes and upswept wing tips* on this large and common Navy and Air Force fighter-bomber; overhead, look for that *deep triangular wing* and comparatively *small tail plane.*

Huge for a carrier-based aircraft, the fighter-bomber version carries 8 tons of munitions, more than the payload of a WWII B-29 Superfortress. Powered by twin Rolls-Royce or General Electric engines, it is nearly as fast as any special-purpose plane designed today. It's the basic interceptor, fighter-bomber, and electronic reconnaissance aircraft for all the U.S. services and more than a dozen foreign countries.

McDonnell Douglas A-4 Skyhawk and TA-4 trainer

Length: 40' (12.2 m)   *Wingspan:* 27'6" (8.38 m)   *Level flight:* 675 mph (1086 km/h) Mach 0.89 at sea level

More than 20 versions, including radar intelligence gathering versions with probes and domes.

Increasingly rare. Look for it near Marine airfields. Note the *refueling probe on the pilot's right, extending forward of the nose* and engine *air intakes above the wing.* Newer models have a distinct *humpback electronic dome on the fuselage.*

A light, single-engine attack plane designed to carry nuclear weapons and penetrate the Soviet Union from naval carriers, the "Bantam Bomber" carries more than 4 tons of armament on a 10-ton airframe. The deep, almost delta, wing was designed to allow it to operate from carriers without a folding wing. Now rare in the Navy, it remains the basic Marine Corps fighter-bomber, until replaced by the AV-8 Harrier.

MILITARY AIRCRAFT

General Dynamics
F-106 Delta Dart

McDonnell Douglas
F-4 Phantom

U.S. AIR FO

MARINES

McDonnell Douglas
A-4 Skyhawk

NAVY

TA-4 Trainer

British Aerospace Hawk, T-54

Length: 36'7" (11.16 m)   *Wingspan:* 30'9" (9.38 m)   *Level flight:* 645 mph (1038 km/h) Mach 0.85 at sea level

Expected to enter U.S. Navy service in 1988. *Small, slim, tandem-seat cockpit canopy flows smoothly into the fuselage* (compare the bumpy canopy on the A-4 Skyhawk trainer); *two small ventral fins; slim swept wings.*

The Royal Air Force's standard jet trainer. First delivered in 1976, the Hawk, with extensive modifications, will replace both the Navy's T-2 Buckeye and the TA-4 Skyhawks. Major advantages include a fuel consumption rate averaging only 40 percent of existing Navy trainers. McDonnell Douglas will be the prime contractor for an expected $2.2 billion worth of T-54s, with British Aerospace providing the complete airframe and Rolls-Royce, the engine.

McDonnell F-101B Voodoo

Length: 67'5" (20.55 m)   *Wingspan:* 39'7" (12.06 m)   *Level flight:* 1220 mph (1963 km/h) Mach 1.85 at altitude

Seen only in Canada. A strikingly *long, thin fuselage* balanced over a *swept wing with strong fairings; a very slim swept tail plane.*

A good aircraft will survive anything, including a canceled mission. The F-101 was designed as a long-range fighter-escort for Strategic Air Command bombers before the introduction of B-52s, but the SAC gave up on that concept before the first plane was delivered in 1957. The trouble-free and reliable design was too good to throw away, and the plane has been variously used as an interceptor, a fighter-bomber and a reconnaissance plane. The few remaining planes are in air defense roles in Canada.

Lockheed F-104 Starfighter

Length: 54'9" (16.69 m)   *Wingspan:* 21'11" (6.68 m)   *Level flight:* 1450 mph (2330 km/h) Mach 2.2 at altitude

Rare. Seen in Canada only. A bizarre combination: *long, needle-nosed fuselage; stubby trapezoid wings; T-tail.*

The first production aircraft with a T-tail, the 1954 Starfighter was built by the thousands and ordered by virtually every U.S. ally. The plane was manufactured under license in Germany, Holland, Belgium, Italy, Canada, and Japan. For many years the hottest aircraft in the world, it set altitude records for airplanes taking off under their own power (118,860 feet, in 1963) and several women's speed records, set by Jacqueline Cochran in 1964. One F-104 was given a complete rocket engine and took off in zero distance in 1963.

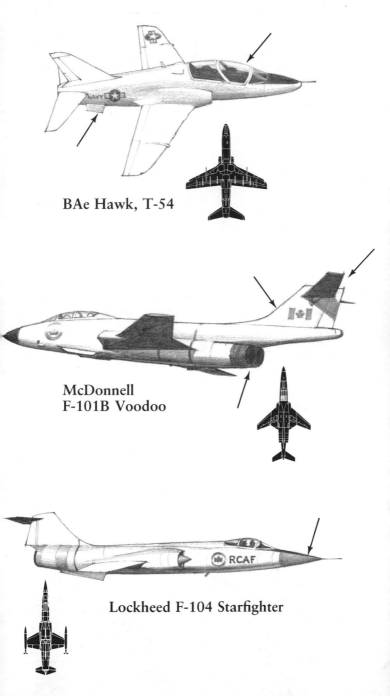

MILITARY AIRCRAFT

BAe Hawk, T-54

McDonnell
F-101B Voodoo

Lockheed F-104 Starfighter

Northrop F-5 Freedom Fighters/Talon T-38 trainer, F-20 Tigershark

Length: 46'–51' (14.0 m–15.5 m)   *Wingspan:* 25'–26' (7.6 m–7.9 m)   *Level flight:* E version, 1060 mph (1706 km/h) Mach 1.6 at altitude

The T-38 version was used for ten years by the USAF Thunderbirds precision flying team at airshows; the fighter-interceptor versions are very rare in the U.S. The *small, oval engine intakes* and the simple, almost *triangular, wing and tail planes* are unique among military aircraft.

More than a thousand T-38s are in use by the Air Force and Navy as trainers, and several thousand versions of the F-5 have been sold with Defense Department subsidies to noncommunist air forces throughout the world. About 100 F-5Es equipped with radar and weapons systems that mimic Russian equipment are based at Nellis Air Force Base, in Nevada, and at Miramar Naval Air Station, in California, where they are used in war games to imitate Russian MiG-21 fighters. F-5s have been manufactured under license in Canada and are in service with the Canadian Defence Force.

General Dynamics F-16 Fighting Falcon

Length: 46'6" (14.2 m)   *Wingspan:* 31' (9.45 m)   *Level flight:* 1300 mph (2092 km/h) Mach 1.96 at altitude

Widely seen. The USAF Thunderbirds have flown the F-16 since 1983. Head on, note the "shark's mouth" air intake and *the drooping tail plane;* in side view, the plane appears to perch on top of the engine and shows a *keel-like stabilizer* aft of the wings; overhead, the *clipped triangular wing and tail planes* are diagnostic.

A bundle of graphite-epoxy wrapped around an afterburning turbofan jet engine, the F-16 started out as an experimental design to test lightweight construction techniques and ended up as the Air Force's choice as a combat fighting machine over battlefield areas. Since its adoption in 1975, the Air Force has turned it into a fighter-bomber and long-range interceptor, adding to its weight and cutting its maneuverability.

McDonnell Douglas–Northrop F-18 Hornet

Length: 56' (17.07 m)   *Wingspan:* 37'6" (11.43 m)   *Level flight:* 1190 mph (1915 km/h) Mach 1.8 at altitude

Rare. Its numbers in the 1980s will depend on procurement of this controversial aircraft. On the flight line, *half-round air intakes and twin tail fins that lean out noticeably;* overhead, stubby, *clipped triangular wings and swept tail fins.*

Intended as the single-pilot alternative to the expensive two-man F-14, the F-18 will be adopted by the Navy as its primary carrier-based fighter. If there were no two-seat versions—though there are for training purposes—it would separate easily from the other twin-tailed fighters, the Air Force F-15 Eagle and the Navy F-14 Tomcat (next entries), in side view. It is the only one of the three with a needle nose and a noticeable offset in the leading edge of the wings.

MILITARY AIRCRAFT

Northrop
F-5 Freedom
Fighter

Talon T-38
Trainer

F-20

F-16B

General
Dynamics F-16

McDonnell
Douglas F-18

NAVY

McDonnell Douglas F-15 Eagle

Length: 63′8″ (19.42 m)   *Wingspan:* 42′8″ (13.0 m)   *Level flight:* 1650 mph (2655 km/h) Mach 2.5 at altitude

Increasingly common. *Massive rectangular engine air intakes;* wing and tail planes of *multifaceted geometry;* and *twin vertical tail fins.*

This airplane gives the impression of a great deal of mechanism crammed close together. The small cockpit seems to bubble up higher and more abruptly than on any modern jet fighter. A training version has two seats in tandem. The appearance of a large amount of engine and a small amount of airframe is indicative of the plane's performance: It is faster than all but the most advanced Russian MiG-25s and much more maneuverable than they are at high speeds. May be seen with a bulge along the outside of each engine housing, indicating removable fuel tanks. These give the plane a maximum range of nearly 4000 miles.

Grumman F-14 Tomcat

Length: 61′10″ (18.85 m)   *Wingspan:* fully spread, 64′1″ (19.5 m); fully swept, 38′2″ (11.63 m)   *Level flight:* 1560 mph (2510 km/h) Mach 2.35 at altitude

A complex variable-wing plane. On first view, compare the F-15 Eagle and F-18 Hornet before deciding; on the flight line, *twin tail fins angle out slightly, rectangular air intakes angle inward at the top.* When the wings are extended at takeoff and landing, note the *bulky wing roots* housing the variable geometry mechanism.

When the F-111 swept-wing proved much too heavy for carrier basing, the Navy chose the F-14 from a design competition. Separating Navy F-14s from Air Force F-15s by service markings will become increasingly difficult as planes are stripped of any distinctive painted markings that would make them identifiable on radar. F-15 Eagles have a smaller bubble canopy for a single pilot, whereas the F-14 carries a pilot and a radar intercept officer under a longer canopy.

General Dynamics F-111, FB-111, and EF-111A

Length: 73′6″ (22.40 m)   *Wingspan:* fully spread, 63′ (19.2 m), fully swept, 31′11″ (9.74 m)   *Level flight:* 1650 mph (2655 km/h) Mach 2.4 at altitude

On the ground or near the base, *thin swept wings* jut out of the *bulky wing roots* housing the variable geometry mechanism; in side view, note a curious asymmetrical sculpting of the nose.

The F-111, developed as a supersonic fighter-bomber, has evolved into a less common medium-range bomber (FB-111) and, in the EF configuration, as a radar suppressor and target locater. The rare EFs are distinguished by an electronic pod in the upper tail fin. What we have here is essentially a half-sized B-1 bomber (or perhaps the B-1 is an oversized F-111). Although one is unlikely to see an F-111 in the fully swept mode (the plane will be very high and going very fast) it would be separable from delta-wing planes by the notched effect where the wing meets the tail plane and by the clipped-off tail planes.

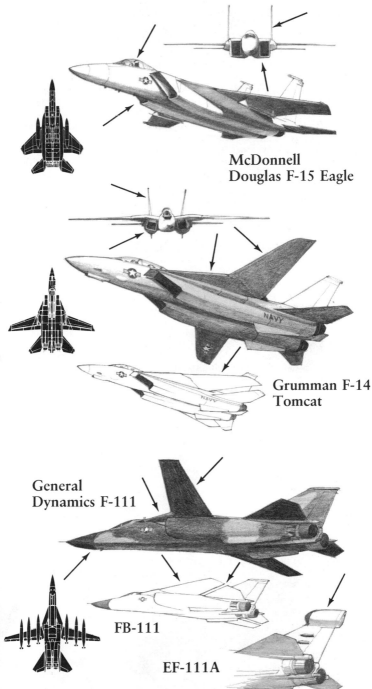

MILITARY AIRCRAFT

McDonnell
Douglas F-15 Eagle

Grumman F-14
Tomcat

General
Dynamics F-111

FB-111

EF-111A

Rockwell B-1

Length: 143′ (43.58 m) *Wingspan:* fully spread, 137′ (41.75 m); fully swept, 78′ (23.77 m) *Level flight:* 1454 mph (2339 km/h) Mach 2.19 at altitude; subsonic at sea level

Huge, the size of a Boeing 707 or a stretched DC9 Super 80, with *four engines mounted in pairs near the wing roots; wings extend for landing and takeoff, sweep back for operational flight;* a sculptural quality to the drooping nose and fuselage-to-wing area; two *beardlike winglets under the "chin"* and a *bulletlike "closeout" fairing to the tail end of the fuselage.*

This plane will be produced in small numbers, but will attract attention by its size alone. You are unlikely to see it except with the wings fully extended unless you are near desert testing areas, where it will be executing supersonic, low-level maneuvers. On the ground, its massive, tall landing gear gives it a birdlike pose.

Lockheed U-2, TR-1

Length: 49′7″ (15.11 m) *Wingspan:* 80′ (24.38 m) *Cruising speed:* 460 mph (740 km/h) Mach 0.69 at altitude

Very unusual configuration. *Single jet engine* and *80-foot wingspan are unique.* The *sensor pods on the wings are integral,* not mounted on pylons. Some appear in civilian dress as research aircraft. Mission pods vary.

The U-2, first flown in 1955, continues to be produced as a platform for aerial observation from the ordinarily safe height of 80,000 feet or more. In addition to the Air Force, NASA and other civilian agencies fly them for high-altitude scientific research. New versions, equipped with side-looking radar and laser equipment for selecting targets and guiding missiles and bombs to them are designated TR-1. Large, wing-mounted fuel tanks give the U-2 the appearance of a twin jet when seen overhead.

Lockheed SR-71A Blackbird

Length: 107′5″ (32.74 m) *Wingspan:* 55′7″ (16.95 m) *Level flight:* at least 2310 mph (3717 km/h) Mach 3.4 at altitude

Rare. Usually at Beale Air Force Base, in California. *Huge, the size of a jet liner; bizarre shape; twin engines mounted on delta wing; inward-leaning twin tail fins.* Painted *dark blue,* but appears black at a distance.

You'll probably never see one in the air, just when it's landing and taking off. With a service altitude of well over 80,000 feet and a speed faster than a military rifle bullet, it's not meant to be seen. The SR-71's mission is data acquisition, including mapping and communications surveillance. However, it has certain qualities similar to those desired from the proposed Stealth bomber, including rounded surfaces wherever possible to scatter radar reflections; the blue paint, intended to diffuse the heat generated by its high speed, is also the worst radar reflector.

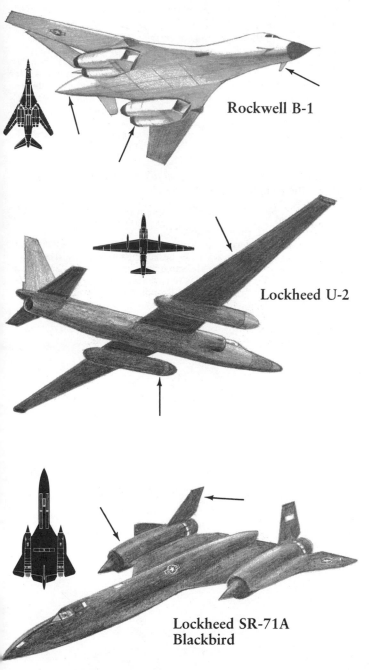

MILITARY AIRCRAFT

Rockwell B-1

Lockheed U-2

Lockheed SR-71A
Blackbird

Douglas A-3 Skywarrior

Length: 76'4" (23.27 m)   *Wingspan:* 72'6" (22.1 m)   *Level flight:* 610 mph (981 km/h) Mach 0.79 at sea level

Scarce. Note the long, thin *swept wings with engines mounted well forward.* The wings enter the fuselage *without fairings.*

The A-3 was designed in 1952 as the first all-jet nuclear bomber to fly from a carrier deck and is the heaviest carrier-borne aircraft in any navy. But, as bombs got lighter and aircraft more sophisticated, it has been relegated entirely to mission support, either as a pure in-air refueling tanker or as a combination tanker–radar suppression plane. A few of the originals are seen near naval air bases, where they are used in multiengine training.

Lockheed S-3 Viking

Length: 53'4" (16.26 m)   *Wingspan:* 68'8" (20.93 m)   *Level flight:* 506 mph (814 km/h) Mach 0.76 at altitude

Note the *twin jet engines pylon-mounted down and forward of the wing* and the *unswept wings;* overhead, it has noticeably *greater wingspan than length.*

When seen on alert, a long magnetic detecting boom extends to 15 feet behind the tail. A carrier-based antisubmarine-warfare craft with a crew of four, it has the same mission as the land-based, turboprop Orion P-3 Electra. It is remarkably maneuverable for a reconnaissance aircraft, capable of dropping to sea level from 30,000 feet in two minutes. In addition to magnetic detection, the S-3 has side- and forward-looking radar and infrared capacity. Conversions to passenger and cargo uses for delivery to aircraft carriers are coming into service.

MILITARY AIRCRAFT

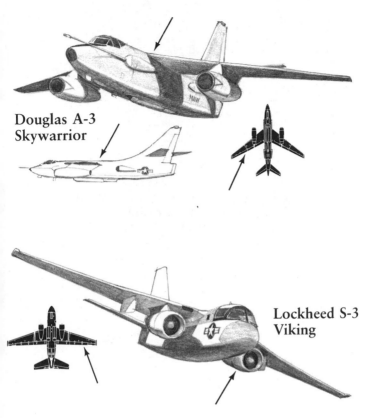

Douglas A-3
Skywarrior

Lockheed S-3
Viking

Lockheed C-5A Galaxy

Length: 247'10" (75.54 m)   *Wingspan:* 222'8" (67.87 m)
Cruising speed: long range, 518 mph (833 km/h) Mach 0.78 at
altitude

Uncommon. Compare the C-141 StarLifter (next entry) before
deciding. *Massive fuselage* with *high wing* and *T-tail. Four turbofan engines* (noticeably larger in front, tapering to aft); overhead,
compare the Boeing 747 silhouette (page 162).

The largest, and certainly the loudest, aircraft in North America,
the C-5A is an awesome sight on takeoff, with flaps fully extended
and four engines generating more than twice the noise of a Boeing
747. Viewed overhead, it can be distinguished from the 747 (both
have engines that taper noticeably from front to back, unlike the
C-141's) by the wing shape: There is very little fairing, or widen-
ing, of the wing root on the C-5A as it enters the fuselage.

Lockheed C-141A StarLifter (and stretched C-141B)

Length: C-141A, 145' (44.2 m); C-141B, 168'4" (51.28 m)
Wingspan: both models, 159'10" (48.74 m)   *Cruising speed:*
495 mph (796 km/h) Mach 0.75 at altitude

Based nationwide. On the ground, one of two *high-wing, four-
jet, T-tail* planes in North America. See the similar C5-A Galaxy
(previous entry) for comparison. Confusing overhead, but the
bulges under and just aft of the *moderately swept wings* house the
landing gear.

The Air Force's basic cargo and passenger aircraft, the jumbo-
jet-sized C-141 differs from all commercial four-engine jets by the
combination of the high wing and T-tail. Within a few years, all
the C-141s will be stretched into the B versions, which also have a
domed fairing to house an in-flight refueling receptacle on the top
of the fuselage just aft of the cockpit. Like many commercial jets,
the original C-141 had more lifting capacity than cabin capacity;
the same solution so common in airliners, stretching, though it improved total load capacity, did not solve the problem created by
the narrow cross section of the fuselage, which keeps it from carrying bulky items, such as full-sized tanks.

Boeing B-52 Stratofortress

Length: 157'7" (48 m)   *Wingspan:* 185' (56.39 m)   *Level flight:*
650 mph (1046 km/h) Mach 0.98 at altitude

Eight engines are carried in pairs below and forward of the
wings' leading edges. Overhead, the contrails frequently show the
eight exhausts, but note the *unfaired swept wings, illusion of four
engines;* on the flight line, *droopy-winged.*

Of the more than 550 B-52s built in the 1950s and early 1960s,
347 remain in service. Current models may show a bulge below the
cockpit, housing forward-looking radar or low-light television.
Many carry two air-to-surface missiles between the outboard engines and the wing tips. In a few years, many will be seen with a
dozen wing-mounted, short-range Cruise missiles. Some current
models may be carrying a number of wing-mounted rockets intended to divert heat-seeking surface-to-air antiaircraft missiles.

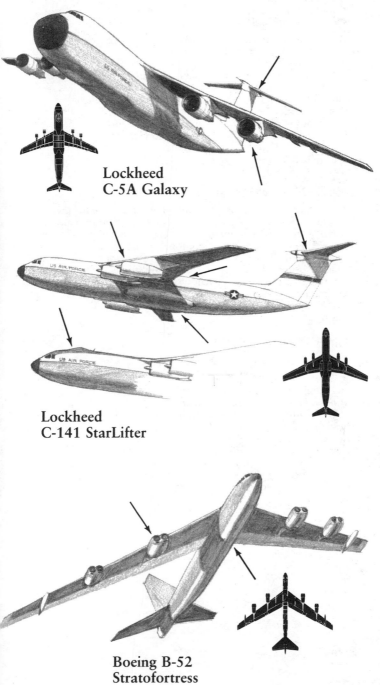

MILITARY AIRCRAFT

Lockheed
C-5A Galaxy

Lockheed
C-141 StarLifter

Boeing B-52
Stratofortress

Lear Fan 2100

Length: 40'7" (12.37 m)   *Wingspan:* 39'4" (11.99 m)   *Cruising speed:* 322 mph (518 km/h)

Under development in 1984. Butterfly V-shaped tail with large ventral fin; rear-mounted twin turbine engines power a single pusher propeller; slim, unswept, tapering wings.

One of the most bizarre airplane designs since the "Flying Wing" of WWII. A seven-to nine-passenger, crew of one, business "jet." Included here with canard-type pusher propellers because, although it lacks the forward small wing, the Lear Fan 2100 is clearly of the revolutionary movement. Problems with the pressurized section of the aircraft have delayed certification.

Avtek 400

Length: 34' (10.36 m)   *Wingspan:* 34' (10.36 m)   *Cruising speed:* estimated 300 mph (483 km/h)

Combines *tall tailfin without tail plane, small canard wing above cockpit, and low main wing with tipsails and twin pusher engines.*

First flight expected in late 1984; first deliveries expected in late 1985. Takes the standard turbopropeller engine and mounts it backward, finally getting the air intake up in front of the exhaust, where it belonged all the time. Wings and fuselage of composite construction. Design instigated by Al Mooney, who has been designing hot airplanes since the 1920s (see the Culver Cadet, page 45). Carries six to nine passengers; cabin fairly small, less than five feet wide and high.

Gates-Piaggio GP180

Length: 46'6" (14.17 m)   *Wingspan:* 45'5" (13.86 m)   *Cruising speed:* estimated 280 mph (451 km/h)

The only twin pusher with *three lifting surfaces, small, low wing at nose, midmounted conventional wing, and T-tail plane.*

While others push on with composite fuselages or fanjet engines pushing radical propellers, the Gates-Piaggio takes a standard and proven aluminum fuselage and wing design and a proven turbocharged piston engine. First prototypes will fly in Italy in 1985. Crew of two; seats seven in a cabin 5 feet 9 inches (1.75 m) high, 6 feet (1.82 m) wide. New-technology composites used only in forward wing and nose cone, engine nacelles, and tail.

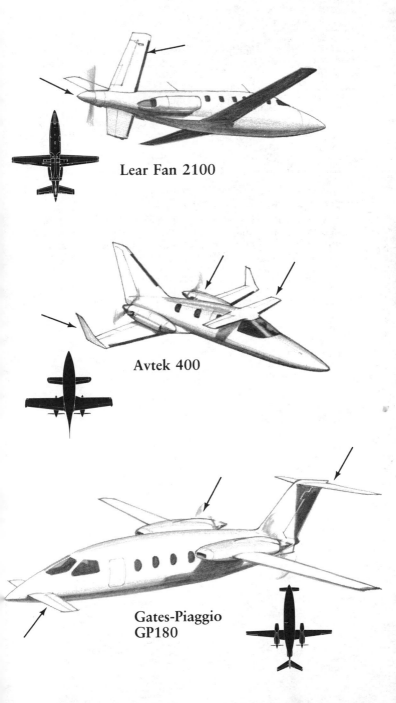

NEW GENERATION PUSHER-PROP

Lear Fan 2100

Avtek 400

Gates-Piaggio
GP180

OMAC 1

Length: 29'6" (9 m)   *Wingspan:* 38'6" (11.73 m)   *Cruising speed:* estimated 266 mph (428 km/h)

A *single pusher behind a slightly swept wing with huge fairing ("strake") that reaches from cockpit back to the wing; winglets top and bottom; small canard wing mounted through the fuselage; no tail surfaces.*

The Old Man's Aircraft Company flew its prototype OMAC 1 in 1983. A turbocharged piston engine, an existing propeller design, and all-aluminum construction were chosen to simplify achieving federal certification, hoped for by the end of 1984. Will carry seven or eight passengers in a cabin with interior head space of 5 feet 4 inches (1.62 m).

Beechcraft Starship I

Length: 46'1" (14.05 m)   *Wingspan:* 54' 6½" (16.66 m)   *Cruising speed:* estimated more than 400 mph (644 km/h)

Unmistakable: *rear wings set below the fuselage* with 7-foot 9-inch tipsails canted inward, no tail (but a small ventral fin), twin pushing propellers. Forward wing is linked to the flap system and swings from a slight forward sweep on takeoff and landing to a strong rearward sweep at cruising speeds.

First flown (as an 85 percent prototype) in 1983. Planned as an executive plane with seating for seven plus a galley; or seats eight to ten in airliner configuration. Controls and cockpit configuration deliberately similar to the Beech King Air 200. Pressurized cabin measures 5 feet 6 inches from side to side and floor to ceiling. Fanjet engines, mounted on top of the wing, drive twin pushing propellers.

NEW GENERATION PUSHER-PROP

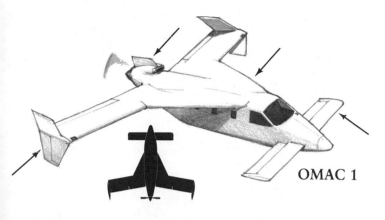

OMAC 1

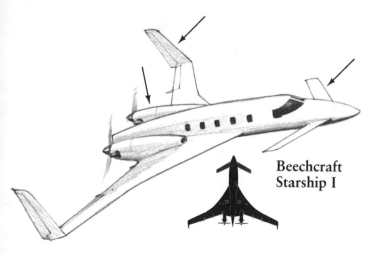

Beechcraft
Starship I

Further Reading

The standard works on aircraft are the annual issues of *Jane's All the World's Aircraft.* Back copies are often available in public libraries or used book stores. The annual *Jane's* includes only the aircraft being built that year, so back copies are necessary to get their wonderful detailed information on obsolete aircraft.

Of encyclopedias, the best of all is the *Encyclopedia of the World's Commercial and Private Aircraft,* compiled by David Mondey and published in the United States by Crown Publishers. It is thorough and includes nearly half of the commercial and private airplanes in this field guide.

There is no single source for encyclopedic information on military aircraft. The best series covering military aircraft of various countries and services is Bill Gunston's work for Salamander Press. His *Illustrated Guide to the Modern U.S. Air Force* is excellent. For the U.S. Navy, an occasional publication, *The Ships and Aircraft of the U.S. Fleet,* by Norman Polmar, is definitive, but it is also 90 percent ships. The current twelfth edition is available from the Naval Institute Press, Annapolis, Maryland.

Keeping track of changes in the civil and military airfleet is best done by referring to the latest issue of *Jane's All the World's Aircraft* or by looking up the *Jane's* supplements in the *Air Force Journal,* which publishes a supplement provided to it by *Jane's.* (Public relations officers for the U.S. Department of Defense will refer you to the *Air Force Journal,* a private publication, before recommending their own government material.)

For readers interested in the price of airplanes, two major American publications, *Plane & Pilot Magazine* and *Flying,* issue buyer's guides each year, and these are available at newsstands that handle the parent magazines. Both *Plane & Pilot Magazine*'s "Aircraft Directory" and the annual *Flying Buyers Guide* have information on sailplanes and home-builts, in addition to production airplanes.

Acknowledgments

The authors are particularly grateful to Mark Foster, who sacrificed many a summer day and fall weekend to search out photographs and specifications for the most obscure aircraft. The aircraft manufacturers were generous with photographs and data sheets, although a few were puzzled as to why anyone would be interested in last year's models.

Historical data are the most difficult to recover in a forward-thinking industry, but two companies deserve special admiration for their excellent archives—Grumman Aerospace of Long Island, New York, and the Lockheed Corporation of California. Two national organizations, the American Aviation Historical Society of Santa Ana, California, and the Antique/Classic Division of the Experimental Aircraft Association of Oshkosh, Wisconsin, were generous in searching out back copies of their publications and forwarding them promptly. Of the many clubs devoted to the restoration and admiration of classic airplanes, the National WACO Club of Hamilton, Ohio, was particularly helpful in sorting out the mysteries of that delightful family of biplanes.

As we look over shelves holding dozens of linear feet of books on aviation and piles of magazines and newsletters, we are reminded of how many people have spent so much time and effort at chronicling the history of aviation. If this *Field Guide* encourages the reader to sample a fraction of the varied literature, some of our debt to those authors and organizations will be repaid.

Index

211